SUMNER COUNTY, TENNESSEE

Abstracts of Will Books 1 and 2
(1788-1842)

Compiled by
EDYTHE RUCKER WHITLEY

CLEARFIELD

Reprinted for
Clearfield Company, Inc. by
Genealogical Publishing Co., Inc.
Baltimore, Maryland
1995, 1999

Originally published: Nashville, Tennessee, 1956
Reprinted: Genealogical Publishing Co., Inc.
Baltimore, 1978, 1980
Reproduced, with permission of the author,
from the original mimeograph edition
Library of Congress Catalogue Card Number 78-60960
International Standard Book Number 0-8063-0825-7

PREFACE

Before 1796 Tennessee was a part of North Carolina.

In 1783 there was only one county in the Cumberland Settlement or Miro District of North Carolina. In 1786 this territory was divided into three counties, Tennessee, Dividson, and Sumner.

Sumner County was erected on November 17, 1786, by an Act of the Legislature of North Carolina. It was formed from a part of Davidson County and was named in honor of General Jethro Sumner, a gallant officer of the Revolution.

Colonel Isaac Bledsoe built a fort or station about a quarter of a mile west of Bledsoe's Lick; and his brother, Colonel Anthony Bledsoe, built a fort two and one-half miles north of the Lick and called it "Greenfield." Colonel Anthony Pledsoe also owned land in Kentucky and in the Holston. The Bledsoes, although descended from Virginia stock, came from North Carolina. Asher and others built a fort a little southeast of Gallatin. Forts were also built by John Morgan, Major James White, Colonel Sanders, Jacob Zigler, Captain Joseph Wilson, Kasper Mansker, Hamilton, and others.

The first court of Sumner County was held on the first Monday in March 1787, at the house of John Hamilton, at Station Camp Creek, about five miles from Gallatin.

On April 20, 1796, the Legislature of Tennessee passed an Act appointing commissioners to select a site for the seat of government. Section 3 of this Act provided that the town should be called "Ca Ira" which name soon became "Cairo," and it was incorporated November 5, 1815. On October 2, 1797, this Act was repealed and another Act passed appointing another commission to select the county site, to buy land, erect a Court House, Prison, and Stocks. This Act was repealed on October 26, 1799, and Sumner County was reduced to its constitutional limits. On November 6, 1804, an Act was passed by the Legislature to provide for a County Seat and building and that the town should be called "Gallatin," in honor of Albert Gallatin, Secretary of the Treasury of the United States.

In February 1802, the site of Gallatin was purchased from James Trousdale who served under General Francis Marion and commanded a company of North Carolina Militia which guarded the jail at Hillsboro and was present at the siege at Charleston. He died 1818 age 82 years and buried near Gallatin. His wife was Elizabeth Dobbins. The Court House was completed in 1803.

On the same day, October 26, 1799, Wilson County and Smith County were carved from a part of Sumner County. The first settlement in that part called Wilson County is accredited to have been at Drake's Lick on the Cumberland River and was made in 1797 by John Foster and William McClain. Smith County was named in honor of General Daniel Smith, a pioneer, surveyor, Secretary of the Southwest Territory, and United States Senator, succeeding Andrew Jackson.

Early settlers in Sumner County came mostly from Watauga, North Carolina, and Virginia; a few came from Pennsylvania and South Carolina; many of them from the battlefields of the revolution. Some of them had seen active service at King's Mountain.

The history of Sumner County actually begins about 1779 when a settlement of a dozen families was formed near Bledsoe's Lick. The winter of 1779-80 brought many new settlers. It continued to flow although there were many dangers and hardships which the people had to encounter. Many of these first-comers were killed by the Indians. Cisco, in his "Historic Sumner County, Tennessee," gives a list of those known to have lost their lives at the hands of savage Indians.

The early records of Sumner County have fortunately been preserved. They reveal the missing link in many a lineage. The abstracts herein are invaluable inasmuch as Sumner County was the crossroads to western migration for many families, who either tarried for a short time, or whose children moved on into various directions with the trend of migration.

These abstracts are, therefore, some of the most valuable genealogical material in Tennessee.

Edythe Whitley
Edythe Whitley
Genealogist-Historian

October 19, 1956

SUMNER COUNTY, TENNESSEE

Will Book 1. Abstracts

John TATHUM - January 1788 - John Luthin of Washington County,
Virginia appoints Isaac Bledsoe of Sumner Co., N.C., lawful attorney
John Provine of Sullivan Co. buys land in Sumner Co. on Station Camp
Creek containing 640 acres; witnessed by D. Hay Anthony Bledsoe.
Proved July 18, 1788. (BL)

Thomas MARTIN (MASTIN) Peter Looney, Robert Looney - 1788 -
Condition is that Thomas Martin is appointed Sheriff of Sumner Co.
and Collector of said county, etc. David Shelby was witness. (P.1)

Anthony BLEDSOE - July 20, 1788 Will - Proved October 18, 1788.
Lands in Kentucky, to be sold. Likewise lands on Holston. Children
to be educated equally. Lands to be divided equally between children.
Daughters small tract of land. Wife to keep negroes. Appoints
brother Isaac Bledsoe and Col. Daniel Smith, executors with wife Mary
Bledsoe executrix. Witnessed by James Clendening, Thomas Murry and
Hugh Rogan. (P.2)

James BOSLEY - March 17, 1789 Deed - James Bosley of Davidson
County, N.C., for 20 pounds sold to David Shelby of Sumner Co. a
mulatto boy named Nick. Witnessed by George Blackmon and Stokley
Donelson (Donalson). (P.2)

James DOUGLAS, Joshua HADLEY, Elmon DOUGLAS, Charles CARTER,
Edward DOUGLAS, Robert MONTGOMERY - 1789 Bond - Condition. James
Douglas appointed Sheriff. (P.2)

Thomas KENNEY - 1789 - October 12 Thomas Kenney sold to Zachariah
Green of Sumner Co. for 16 pounds Virginia money household furniture.
Witnessed by: James McKain, Jr., Charles Carter. (P.3)

Arthur GILBREATH - 1789 - November 18 Deed. Arthur Gilbreath of
Hawkins Co., N.C., for the good will and appreciation I bear unto
Thomas Sharp of Davidson County, N.C., as well as certain wish and con-
fidence I have reposed in him without other good purposes, me hereunto
moving --- to recover notes from James McKain dated December 26, 1782
and September 28, 1782. Wit: Robert Stewart. (P.4)

Henry RUYLE (RULE) - February 16, 1790 Will - Catherine Ruyle the
plantation and household goods and to raise my young children, cows,
horse, etc. Eldest son Henry Ruyle 5 shillings on being provided for
before. Son Andrew Ruyle 5 shillings his being provided for before.
Sons John Ruyle, Solomon Ruyle, Moses Ruyle, Aaron Ruyle, and Peter
Ruyle the plantation and land whereon I now live, after the marriage or
decease of my wife. Peter Ruyle my son being the youngest may have the
cleared land. Daughter Mary CRAVINS 5 shillings she being already
provided for. Daughter Magdalon JONES 5 shillings she being already

- 1 -

provided for. Daughter Margaret Ruyle 5 shillings she being already
provided for. Daughter Elizabeth Ruyle the same. Daughter Delia
COTES the same. Wife CATHERINE and son John executors and executrix.
Wit: N. Phillips, Jno. Cravins, Edward Jones. Proved 1790 July. (P.4)

Abraham SANDERS - 1789 Deed - Robert Desha both of Sumner Co.,
N. C., a negro. Witnessed by David Wilson and George McWhirter. (P.6)

Alexander DUN (DUNN) - May 1790 Deed - He appoints Joseph McKelworth attorney to adjust and settle accounts more especially to recover
a legacy which fell to me by heirship of my mother's death which I do
fully authorize him to recover. Wit: Benount Searcy (intended for
Bennett Searcy I think). Proved 1790. (P.6)

John WILLIAMS & Benjamine WILLIAMS^o9 1790 - July 13, 1790, Elmon
Douglas 200 pounds Virginia currency in full for negro boys named
Arthur and Benjamine. Wit: Edward Douglas, William Frazor, Sion
Peny. (P.7)

Simpson HART - February 23, 1790 Will - Brother-in-law Lawrence
Thompson right to one thousand acres of land in District of Kentucky
which my father left me in his will and which land was to be my own
choosing. To my four youngest brothers and sisters Cumberland Hart,
Thomas Hart, Richard Hart, and Green Hart, Mary Hart, and China Hart
one half of remainder of my real estate in land lying in State of
North Carolina and in State of Virginia. In case my brother or
sister should die under age it shall be divided among the surviving.
To my sister Kiziah THOMPSON's five children Richard Lawrence
THOMPSON, SARAH FANNY THOMPSON, Nathaniel Hart THOMPSON, China
Burton THOMPSON, Azaniah Thompson THOMPSON to remainder of my real
estate lying in the State of North Carolina and Virginia, which land
I am entitled to by virtue of will of my father Nathaniel Hart.
Nominates: Jesse Oldham, William Bushm, Nicholas George of District
of Kentucky executors. Wit: N. Phillips, James Whitsett, Hugh
Tennon, John Whitsett. (P.7)

Hugh McCARY of Mercer County, Kentucky - September 1789 Deed -
Sells Kasper Mansker negroes. Wit: Andy Jackson, Charles Hamman.(P.9)

Nathaniel PARKER - September 20, 1790 Deed - Nathaniel Parker
of Hampshire Co., Virginia, appoints Elmon Douglas of Sumner Co.,
N.C., attorney to act for him in sale and act in all matters in his
interest. Wit: Edward Douglas. (P.9)

William EDWARDS - November 1789 Deed - Sold to Elmon Douglas,
negroes. Wit: Sion Perry, Reuben Douglas. (P.10)

Isaac BLEDSOE - September 1790 Deed - Negro from Thankful Hall
the admr. of Wm. HALL. Wit: John Neely and Hugh Rogan. (P.10)

John DAWSON - December 17, 1790 - Elmon Douglas of Sumner Co.
from Dawson, negroes. Wit: Edward Douglas, Jno. Hyman, Thomas
Christman. (P.10)

Alexander CROMWELL - January 1, 1791 Deed - Sells to Joseph Desha, negroes. (P.11)

John D. HANNAH - August 14, 1790 Deed - Negroes from Hannah to Isaac Bledsoe. Wit: Peter LOONEY. Robert LOONEY. (P.11)

Pearce WALL - January 1, 1791 - Bill of Sale for negroes to Isaac BLEDSOE. Wit: G. Winchester. J. Winchester. (P.12)

Edward TINNON - November 5, 1790 Will - Wife Elizabeth. Daughter Patty. Other children not called by name. Appoints wife and Benj. Williams exec. and execx. of said will. Wit: William Wilson and Wm. Newton. Proved January 13, 1791. (P.12)

Lawrence THOMPSON - December 13, 1790 - Lawrence Thompson of Sumner County, State of N.C., sold to Azaniah Thompson and John Whitsett of Summer Co. a horse, colt, negroes and H.H.Goods. Wit: James Bone, John Jones, Robert Donalson. (P.13)

Joseph WALLACE - August 1789 Bill of Sale - For negro woman to (does not say to whom) Wit: G. Hamilton, James Wilson. (P.14)

Silas McBEE - October 2, 1790 Bill of Sale - Negroes to Thomas Hendricks. Wit: Edward Hogin, Obediah Terril. (P.14)

Alexander ROBINSON - July 28, 1791 Will- Wife Mary land I live on, etc., 2,000 acres of land on north fork of Duck River about five miles from the mouth to be equally divided among my five eldest children, Viz: Jane Robinson, David Robinson, James Robinson, Elizabeth Robinson and Mary Robinson. Youngest daughter Catherine Robinson shall have home plantation after the rest are come of age. Appoints wife Mary with James McCauliston and Azariah Thompson sole executors. Wit: James Whitsett and Thomas Tennon. (P.14)

Ruffin DELOACH - August 11, 1791 Bill of Sale - To Michael Shavin. Wit: David Wilson, Pearce Wall. (P.15)

Richard STROTHER - August 11, 1791 Bill of Sale - Negroes to Michael Shavin. Wit: David Wilson and Pearce Wall. (P.16)

Ruffin DELOACH - August 24, 1791 Bill of Sale - To Michael Shavin, negroes. (P.16)

John SADLER - 1791 Bill of Sale - For negroes to Joseph McELWORTH. (P.17)

Page BALLEW - September 26, 1791 Bill of Sale - Negroes to Peter Lum and John Pullen. Wit: James Franklin and Frances Harney. (P.17)

John SHAVIN - June 9, 1791 Will - Elizabeth Hachn (?) should have a certain tract of land on Drakes Creek 100 acres adjoining Catron and Carr. Frances CATRON should give all papers, etc., to Elizabeth HACKER (HARKER). Peter Shavin to have all that is in his hands. Wit: John Hutchison, Joseph Pryor, Thomas Lanner. (P.18)

John SCOTT - June 27, 1792 Attorney - John Scott of Fayette County, Kentucky, makes Landon Carter of Davidson County, N&nG, his attorney to receive land deed for lands on Spencers Creek from Sampson Williams. Wit: O. Williams. Presley Park. (P18)

Michael SHAVIN - February 11, 1789 Will - Proved January 1793. Wife Catherine, brother John Shavin's oldest son John all residue of real and personal property. Appoints David and John Wilson Executors. Wit: James Rice, William Wilson. (P19)

Isaac BLEDSOE - 1791 Will - Daughter Peggy Bledsoe. Daughter Sally Bledsoe. Daughter Polly Bledsoe. Son Anthony Bledsoe. Son Isaac Bledsoe. Child whereof my wife is now with. Wife Katy Bledsoe. Appoints wife Katy, Anthony Bledsoe, Daniel Smith and George Winchester executors. Wit: John Desha, Jesse Hughes, Thomas Peel, James Lunn, and Michael Shavin. CODICIL. Son William Lytle Bledsoe. Anthony Bledsoe named as Executor is dead and James Winchester is appointed in his place. Wit: J. Winchester, G. Winchester. (P.19)

James McCALLISTER - December 18, 1792 - James McCallister of Mercer County, Kentucky appoints John Robinson of Mercer Co, Ky. attorney to sell property in Sumner Co, N. C. (P.23)

Cathr. SHELBY - March 13, 1793 - Widow, of Sullivan Co. appoints David Shelby of Sumner Co. attorney to attend to business of her dec'd husband Evan Shelby and also for the children of the deceased. Wit: John Shelby, Jr, James McKain. (P24)

David LOONEY - October 1, 1793 Power Attorney - To Edward Douglass of Sumner Co. David Looney of Sullivan Co. to convey a tract of land between Lindsey' Bluff and Hogan's Pond adjoining Wm. Cage. Wit: William Prigance, Samuel Cruthers, Hugh Crafford.(P.24)

A. CRUTCHER - April 1793 - A. Crutcher of Tennessee County authorizes David Shelby of Sumner County to handle suit against James McKain for and on account of him the said McKain failing to locate and survey a warrant issued to Thomas Davis for 630 acres agreeable to an article of agreement 13 February 1790. (P.25)

Ephraium PEYTON - May 1794 - Appoints to Lazanus Cotton attorney to attend to a deed. Test: John Cotton. (P.25)

John ODUM - August 22, 1794 - John Odum of the Government of Natchez, appoints James Odum of Cumberland to handle collection for supplies. Wit: Thomas Nicholls. (P.26)

Katy BLEDSOE - 1794 Nuncupative Will - Thomas Bledsoe,deceased, October 3, 1794. The said Thomas Bledsoe being bodily wounded by the Indians at or near Bledsoe's Lick and while lying in a state of dispair called upon Katy Bledsoe and gave the instructions as to his property, divide among his brothers and sisters. Viz: Sally Shelby. Elizabeth Clendening, Rachel Neely, Susanna Penny, Isaac Bledsoe and Prudy Bledsoe. Thomas Bledsoe departed this life on October 3. (P.26)

William REEL - 1794 - Same as above on Thomas Bledsoe's estate.(P.27)

Joseph EVANS - 1794 - Same as above on Thomas Bledsoe's estate.(P.27)

James LAUDERDALE - November 1794 - Of Roetetourt County, Virginia, appoints Peter Looney attorney because he is moving to settle certain matters in Mero Dist., Sumner Co. Wit: Jno. Tarbury, James Lauderdale, John Kindrick. (P.28)

Joseph BARNES - December 17, 1794 Will - Daughter Molly CLAY. Wife Lelah Barnes. Son William Barnes under 21 yrs. Daughter Polly Barnes. Son John Barnes. Daughter Juslan Barnes. Daughter Selah Barnes. Son Kintihen Barnes. Son William Barnes. Daughter Milly Barnes under age. Seven children. Wife and son John Executors. Proved April 15, 1796. Wit: Wm. Cartwright. Jno. Roberts, John Deloch. (P.28)

Isaac BLEDSOE - April 1795 - Isaac Bledsoe of Davidson Co, N.C. bond to James and George Winchester; Condition that Isaac Bledsoe made deed of General warranty all land called Bledsoe's Mill place on Bledsoe's Creek. (P.30)

Lewis MALOON - April 1795 - Lewis Maloon, Bond, to James Campbell. Condition Lewis Maloon to make unto said James Campbell deed for land in Sumner Co. including spring near the Court House road. January 1, 1792. Wit: John Wilson. John Hamilton. (P.31)

John AVENT and John YOUNG - March 13, 1795 Bond - John Avent at his own free will became apprenticed to John Young, blacksmith, to learn the trade of Blacksmith. Withess: Abraham Saunders. John Saunders. (P.32)

A. BLEDSOE - 1795 - Deed to Hugh Rogan for land. Anthony Bledsoe recites himself of Sullivan Co, N.C. (P.33)

Edward DOUGLAS - February 28, 1793 Will - Wife Sarah and to her to dispose of as she thinks proper. Sons Edward Douglas and son Reubin Douglas executors. Wit: John Dawson. Proved October 6, 1795. (P.33)

Thomas EVANS - October 1795 - Thomas Evans of Surry Co, N.C. bound to James Douglas in Sumner Co, N.C., November 20, 1788, condition deed to sd. James for land in East Fork of Station Camp Creek. (P.34)

David LOONEY - 1795 - David Looney of Sullivan Co, N.C., appointed Edward Douglas of Sumner Co. to make a good and sufficient conveyance unto Samuel GRIGG of Clark Co, Ky., for tract of land in Sumner Co. containing 320 acres. Wit: John Donohoo. James Johnston. (P.35)

Charles HARINGTON (HARRINGTON) - September 3, 1794 Will - Charles Narington of Red River in Sumner Co. Son William Harington lands on south side of Cumberland River adjoining Michael Glass and the widow Crutchfield. Son Thomas Harrington lands I now live on. Wife Elizabeth Harrington, etc. Daughter Sarah McMULLIN 5 shillings. Daughter Elizabeth SUTTON 5 shillings. Daughter Susannah HAMPTON 5 shillings. Daughter Rachel WILSON 5 shillings. Wife Elizabeth and son William executors. Wit: John Nusom (?), Ezekiel Bloyd. (P35)

5

Thomas COTTON - February 10, 1794 Will - Priscilla my dearly
beloved wife. Youngest son Sanders Cotton, under age. Daughter
Letha Cotton. Daughter Sarah Cotton. Son Moore Cotton. Son Allin
Cotton. Son Noah Cotton. Son John Cotton. Son Arthur Cotton.
Nine children. (1) Mary CRYER, (2) Moore Cotton, (3) Letha Cotton,
(4) John Cotton, (5) Allen Cotton, (6) Sarah Cotton, (7) Arthur
Cotton, (8) Noah Cotton, (9) Saunders Cotton. Appoints Moore
Cotton, George Penny and Isaac Walton executors. Wit: Abraham
Rogers, Archd. Martin. Isaac Walton. (P.37)

Edward HOWELL - April 1796 - Francis his wife and executrix.
Wit: Mathew Leabry (Seabry) Betsy Douglas. (P.39)

James LAUDERDALE - September 1796 Will - James Lauderdale of
Botetourt Co, Virginia. Appoints eldest son William Lauderdale and
youngest son James Lauderdale and son-in-law JAMES HENRY executors
of said will. My eldest daughter Margaret CAIN, widow and relict
of James CAIN, dec'd. My grandson James MARTIN. My son William
Lauderdale. My son John Lauderdale. My son James Lauderdale. My
daughter Jane CRAWFORD. My daughter Elizabeth MARTIN. My daughter
Mary FRANKLIN. My daughter Annie HENRY. Grandson John MILLS son
of my daughter Elizabeth aforesaid. Witnessed by John Wood, James
Lauderdale and John Mills. My grandson John Lauderdale son of my
youngest son James. (P.39)

Daniel BENTHALL - January 17, 1797 Will - Wife Susannah.
Children to wit: Elizabeth Benthall, Charlotte Benthall, Francis
Benthall, Mary Benthall, Susannah Benthall. James Cryer appointed
executor. Wit: Laban Benthall and Mary Benthall. (P.41)

Robert HOBDAY - 1797 Will - Wife Tolietha (?), youngest son
Richard Hobday. Son John Hobday. Son William Hobday. Son Thomas
Hobday. Daughter Patience Hobday. Daughter Jelitha Hobday.
Daughter Tibatha Hobday. Daughter Elizabeth Hobday. Son Robert
Hobday. Son Edmond Hobday. Daughter Rossy Ann Hobday. Daughter
Hannah Hobday. James Cryer and Moore Cotton Exec. Wit: William
Carr, Peggy Carr, Moore Cotton. (P.42)

Sarah DOUGLAS - January 3, 1797 - Granddaughter Betsy Black-
more, daughter of Thomas and Sarah Blackmore. Grandson James
Blackmore, son of aforesaid. Residue of estate to go to husband
Edward Douglas and be divided as per his will; re deceased. Grandson
Dyllie Douglas, son of Reuben Douglas. Appointed Reuben Douglas,
executor. Wit: Edward Douglas. Wilson Cage. James Cage. (P.43)

Mary HELLM (HELLEN) - 1798 Will - Daughter Sophia's natural
son commonly called James Hellen. Son Jesse. Daughter Sarah WALL-
DRIP. James Winchester executor. Wit: Parel Harpole and Barbney
Harpole. (P.44)

Prince (Pince) WALL - September 1798 Will - Simon Wall. Son
Hugh Wall. James Cryer and John Withers executors. Wit: Richard
Bradley, Kessee Spradling. Thomas Willis. (P.45)

6

Samuel SIMMON - June 15, 1798 Will - To John Montgomery, son, to my old acquaintance William Montgomery, all my land in Kentucky. To my amiable acquaintance MARGARET McClenahan. Margaret daughter of the above said William. Wit: Joseph McCadam. Edward Duncan. Wm. Morehead. (P.45)

Thomas CUMMINGS - December 4, 1798 Will - To my nephew Thomas Cummings and my niece Ann Cummings son and daughter of Frances Cummings in North Carolina. Kind friend William McGready. Friends Robert and John Goudy. Robert and William Anderson executors. Wit: John and Jane Anderson. (P.46)

Borden HAWKINS - October 1798 Will - Brother John Hawkins. Wit: James and Sara Lauderdale. (P.47)

John BRIGANCE - May 28, 1798 Will - Katherine wife. Son John Brigance. Youngest son Charles Brigance. Son James Brigance. Wit: Richard Strother, Joel Dyer, and Taysey Dyer. (P.47)

William BEAKLEY - February 1798 Will - William Beakley. Sons John Peakley and William Beakley. Eldest daughter Sally Beakley. Daughter Nancy Kealey. My daughter Betsy Beakley under age. David Shelby executor. Wit: Thomas Edwards, Richard Hogin. (P.48)

Francis WILLIS - January 1799 Will - Wife Mary Willis. Son Jacob Willis. Daughters Elizabeth and Mary Willis. Mary Willis and William Phillips executors. Wit: William Snoddy, Charles Elliott. (P49)

Ruffin BARROW - July 1799 Will - Mother shall have all and she is appointed executor. Wit: William Barrow, Phasaby Barrow, David Dano. (P.50)

James CHAPMAN - May 1800 Will - Wife Martha. Sons Samuel Chapman, James Chapman, Benjamine Chapman, William Chapman. Daughter Patsy Chapman. Appoints wife and son Alexander and Alexander Anderson executors. Wit: Thomas Campbell, Charles Larenn. (P.51)

John SEAWELL - May 6, 1801 Will - Wife Alsa. All children under age. Children: Hardy Seawell, Polly Seawell, Benjamine Seawell. Wife and brothers William, Benjamine, and Joseph Seawell executors. Wit: Jno. B. Trulock. John Brown. (P.52)

James BLYTHE - 1801 Will - Wife Elizabeth. Son Richard. Son James. Son Andrew. Daughter Anna. Son Samuel. Wants them to use the advice of friend and brother Robert King. Wife Elizabeth and son James and Richard King, executors. Wit: Feyus Sloan and William Anderson. (P.53)

Edward GILES - November 5, 1800 Will - Family Bible to son Nathaniel. Son Eli one cow. Daughter Elizabeth. Son William. Son Josiah. Daughter Rachel. My beloved wife. Daughter Darcus. Wife and son Eli executors. Wit: Patrick Gibson and John B. Gibson. (P.54)

William HAMILTON - November 18, 1801 Will - Wife. Will that my child be educated. Wm. Douglass, Reuben Cage and Wilson Yandell executors. Wit: Benjamine Rawlings. (P.55)

7

Robert TAYLOR - April 15, 1799 Will - Wife Ann. Son Henning
Taylor. Sons Robert, Manoach (Manoah), and Benjamine. Son John.
Daughter Lucy JOINER. Daughter Keziah KEEN. Daughters Elizabeth,
Nancy and Polly Taylor. Wife and son Robert executors. Witness:
Daniel Taylor and Agnes Maglohom. (P.56)

Daniel ROGERS - December 2, 1801 Will - Wife Hannah. Son
Samuel. Son Staunton. Daughters Lucy, Lucretia, and Polly. Son
Jonathan. My brother Grisworth Latimer to be executor. Witness:
Peter Looney and Jona. Latimer, Junior. (P.57)

John WHITWORTH - December 21, 1801 Will - Son James Whitworth.
Daughter Polly HAREFORD. Son Thomas Whitworth. Daughter Patty
SEARCY. Daughter Tobitha HITHLY. My two little sons, Claiborne
and Samuel Whitworth. Wife Elizabeth Whitworth. Wit: Willishean
Bandy, Paran Bandy, and Isaac Lindsey, Jr. (P.59)

Thomas TULLOCK - November 30, 1784 Will - Halifax County,
North Carolina. Copy taken in February, 1802. Thomas Tullock of
the County of Beaufort, State of North Carolina. Wife Susannah
Tullock and John Vincent Tullock the share coming to my son to
be put to interest. Whereas I was appointed guardian to Fanny
Boles, daughter of my sister Sarah Hoskins in consequence of four
hundred Continental dollars came into my hand. Fanny Boles now
residing in Orange Co, N.C. Appoints wife Susannah, James Cole
Mountflorence, Robert Fenner, and Andrew Armstrong executors.
Witness: Eaton Pugh and John Brown, Jr. John Brown made oath in
Halifax Co, N.C., 1785. (P.59)

John DONOHOO - May 1802 Will - Wife Elizabeth. Son John
200 acres on Dry Fork of Bledsoe's Creek. Son William has already
received his. Son Isaac my third son, 200 acres on Beldsoe's Lick.
Son Walter. Son Benjamine. My fourth, fifth and
sixth sons. I give 210 acres of land on Dry Fork of Bledsoe's
Lick. To James and Anthony my seventh and eighth sons lands.
Anthony gets the place whereon I now live. All children not of
age of 21 years. Daughters Kitty HOLMES. Her son John HOLMES
(under age). Appoints son John Donoho, James Ruse, Esqr.,
Archibald Marlin, executors. Wit: James Hollis. John Ferrin
and Arch Marlin. (P.61)

Hugh ELLIOTT - October 17, 1801 Will - To Margaret COWEN's
three sons, Hugh COWEN, James COWEN, and George COWEN. George is
the youngest and under 21 years. Her daughter Margaret COWEN.
Appoints friends John Withers and James Trousdale executors. Wit:
Edwin Gwin, Charles Elliott. (P.63)

William COCHRAN - December 2, 1801 Will - Daughter Anna
Cochran, son Hiram. Daughter Rachell Cochran. Daughter Sally
Cochran. Daughter Julia TAYLOR and also a child my wife Nancy
is now with. Appoints Doctor John Bush, my brother David Cochran,
my brother-in-law William Hubbert, my nephew John Cochran executors. Wit: Robert Bruce, Tabitha Bean, Benjamine Hubbert. (P.64)

8

John McMANNEY - February 18__ - Will. Friend William Man.
Wit: Thomas Murray, Abz King. George Moodril, Charles Polk. (P.65)

Laurence THOMPSON - October 26, 1790 Will - Daughter Sarah
WHITSETT. Granddaughter Sarah WHITSETT. Granddaughter Sarah THOMPSON.
Daughter Zebellon Tinnin. Daughter Mary WHITSETT. Son Azariah
Thompson. Granddaughter Sarah T. THOMPSON. Son Laurence Thompson.
Wit: Thomas Simpson, Alexander Robinson. (P.66)

John ANDERSON - September 13, 1801 Will - Son Robert Anderson.
Son John Anderson. Son William Anderson. Daughter Anderson now
Jane STEWART. Daughters Mary and Elizabeth GOWDY. Mention is made
of the family burying place. Appoints sons Robert and William
executors. Wit: Wm. Bell, James Far. (P.67)

William GALBREATH - 1801 Will - Daughter Ann WEEMS. Wife.
Four sons, Andrew, John, William and Robert. Daughter Catherine.
Wife and son John executors. (P.69)

Ave BLOODWORTH - August 1803 Verbal Will - Brother William
Bloodworth. Mrs. Douglas. Her sister Patsy. Her sister Purity.
Brother Timothy. (P.70)

James GARDNER - July 1803 Will - Son Hezekiah James Gardner.
Wife. Daughter Abigail Gardner. Youngest daughter Elizabeth Gardner.
Daughter Rachel Gardner. Appoints John Sloan and David Henry,
executors. Wit: B. Seawell, Susannah Seawell and Wilson Yandell.
(P.70)

Michael ASBROOKS - December 9, 1803 Will - Wife Ruth and John
Gwin as executors. Son Sterling Irwin. Son Michael. Wit: Edward
Gwin, Robert Smith, Zalima Granger. (P.72)

Robert MARSHALL - November 23, 1803, January 24, 1804 Will -
Wife Christiana. Son William. Wife and son William executors.
Son Robert, Son Isiah, son John, son James Brown Marshall. Agness
Marshall. Daughter Elizabeth. Wit: Issiah More, David Davis,
William Moore. (P.73)

Nathaniel GILMER - not shown Pvd. 1804 Will - Wife Jean dwelling
and orchard and lands. Daughter Sarah Giles. Daughter Mary. Son
Abner plantation I now live on. Daughter Jean. Daughter Elizabeth.
Appoints James Wilson, Zachore Wilson, son of Samuel Wilson executors.
Wit: Mathew Alexander, Zacon Wilson. (P.75)

David WILSON - pvd. 1804 Will - Son William 214 acres land
including Henry's Lick on Ginnon's Creek and 500 acres on Caney Spr. Cr.
a branch of Duck River. Son James 500 acres land on Caney Spring
branch of Duck River. My son-in-law Zachaus Wilson 400 acres land on
Caney Spring Branch of Duck River. My Jonathan Wisdom 500 acres land
on Caney Spring Creek of Duck R. My William Street 500 acres land on
Spring Creek, of Duck River. My son Zacherus plantation I now live on.
My son James. My son David. Daughter Mary 500 acres land on Duck
River. Appoint Son William Wilson and my son Zacheus Wilson exec.
Wit: Zachr Wilson, James S. Wilson. (P.77)

9

Benj. RONEY - _____ - Will - Half brother James Roney son
of James and Susannah Roney. Friends Isaac Stallcup and Richard
Cope executors. Wit: James Haston, James Roney, Sr. No date
shown. (P.79)

John BUNTON - _____ - Will - Wife Elizabeth. Son Joseph.
Daughter Sarah. Son William. Grandson John Kerr. Son Joseph.
Sons Joseph and William, executors. Wit: Patrick Barr, Nancy
Barr. No date shown. (P.80)

Edward GARRETT - _____ - Will - Daughter Charity ELLIS.
Daughter Thomason DIXON. Sons, James, George, William, and
Martin Garrett. My grandson Edward ELLIS and Edward Garrett
son of George Garrett. Son John Garrett the plantation.
Appoints Daniel Oglesby and Shadrack Nye, executors. May 8,
1801. Witness: William Williams, George Chapman, Job Hicks.(P.80)

Thomas TODD - August 18, 1802 Will - Wife Susannah.
Daughter Margaret Todd. Daughter Pennelope Todd. Six children
not named. Henry Belote executor. Wit: Jas. Bently and James
Murrings (?). (P.81)

Alexander ANDERSON - January 27, 1804 Will - Wife Pheby
Anderson my plantation. Two sons (youngest under age). Children
not called by name. Two brothers William and Thomas Anderson,
executors. Wit: William Bruthot, James Brien, Greenbury Grace,
William Gilliham. (P.82)

Robert MOTHERAL - August 29, 1803 Will - My mother Ann
Greer my whole estate. Brother John Motheral and my mother
executors. Wit: Geo. W. Parker, John Douglas. (P.84)

William BROWN - October 12, 1804 Will - Son James. Daughter
Sally BROWN. Son-in-law Thomas ROPER. Son-in-law John Perkerson.
Son Robert Brown. Son Alexander Brown. Son Richard Brown. Son
John Brown (under age 21). Wife Nancy. Son William. Appoints
as executors: James Hart; Arthur Exam, and son James Brown. Wit:
John Tinn. Elisha Cheek. Simon Coal. (P.84)

William BROWN - May 6, 1804 Will - Wife Mary Hundly Brown.
Children: John Henry Brown, Ludisa Brown, Catherine Brown,
William Russell Brown, Samuel Adams Brown, Celia Wilson Brown.
My eldest daughter Tabitha MOORE and son-in-law Armstead Moore.
Probably other children not called by name. Son John Henry Brown
as executor. (P.85)

John HEADON - May 1, 1800 Nuncupative Will - John Headon who
said he was of Christian Co, Kentucky, in his last illness at
Roger Gibson's of Sumner Co, Tenn, where he died. He said his
wife and child then lived in North Carolina in Chatham Co. Signed
Fanny Gibson and Wilson Yandell. (P.86)

James LINSEY - August 6, 1804 Will - Brother Jno. Linsey,
300 acres on Duck River. To Edward McCAFFERTY my nephew son of

Edward MCCAFFERTY my brother-in-law 250 acres land on waters Cathings
Creek on So. side Duck River. To Edward McCafferty my brother-in-law
remainder of property. Appointed John Wilson and Griffith W. Rutherford
Junr. exec. (P.86)

Griffith RUTHERFORD - _____ - Will - Of Rowan Co, North Carolina.
Wife Elizabeth Rutherford. Sons John and Griffith W. Rutherford lands
on Forked Deer River 5,000 acres. My son Griffith Weakley Rutherford.
Daughter Elizabeth, negroes and H.H.goods. Two sons, not called by
name. Appoints John Johnson Sr., and Henry Rutherford, Robert Weakley
and Robert King, executors. (P.87)

Ormon (Armon ?) ALLEN - January 31, 1803, pvd. Ap. 1805 Will -
Wife Elizabeth Allen, plantation, etc. Son Robert Allen, 640 acres on
Mill Creek in Williamson Co, Tenn. Daughters namely Sarah, Sophia,
Ann Charity. Williamson Allen. Appoints Elizabeth Allen and Joseph
Phillips Esqr., and David Beard, Senr., executors. Daughter Ann and
infant. (P.88)

Reuben NORMAN - July 14, 1805 Will - Three eldest sons (Viz)
Ezekiel Norman, Caleb Norman and Reuben Norman. Wife Rachel. Two
youngest sons under age (Viz) Benjamine and John. My daughter Frances
Campbell. My daughter Margaret Moss. My daughter Polly (under age).
Attest, by Ashley Sharp and Margaret Sharp. (P.89)

Samuel ARMSTRONG - January 16, 1806 Will - Wife Magdalan.
Eldest child is not of age. Sister Elizabeth Armstrong. My property
in North Carolina. Wife and Able Brandon and John Knox executors.(P.90)

Robert KING - January 6, 1806 Will - Wife Mary. Son Samuel land I
now live on containing 640 acres. Son William M. King, land I purchased
from Joseph Sloan 120 acres. Son Davis King, remainder of land upon
which I now live including graveyard and orchard. Daughter Rebecca King.
Daughter Elizabeth King. My brother James King and others on Elk
River. Daughter Rhoda King. Son Richard King and son William M. King
to be executors. Attested by: William Anderson and Samuel M. McCorkle.
(P.92)

John COOK - October 28, 1805 Will - Wife Librey Cook, all my
estate. My daughter Charlotte Cook. Son Nazarith Cook. Son Augustine
Cook. Four youngest children, namely: Clary Cook, Polly Cook, John
Cook, Betsy Cook. My wife and my brother Joel Cook to be executors.
Wit: Isaac Walton, Samuel Tinnon, Benjamine Rice. (P.93)

John HASSELL - January 27, 1806 Will - Wife Peggy. Sons: Jordan
Hassell, Prestley Hassell, John Page Hassell. Daughters: Charlotte
Hassell, Harriett Hassell, Sally Hassell. Appoints Reuben Douglas and
my brother Abraham Hassell, executors. Wit: Wm. Edwards Jr., Richard
Edwards, and Moses Hardin. (P.94)

Elias MORRISSON - September 24, 1805 Will - Wife Mary. Sons
John and Samuel the plantation whereon I live. Daughters Jane and
Margaret Morrisson. My brother-in-law James Stewart executor. Wit:
Thomas Donnell and Joseph Robb. (P.95)

11

Absolum HALL - February 12, 1806 Will - Rachel. Sons James
and David Hall, executors. Son Stephen Hall. Son Absolum Hall.
Daughter Franky Hall. Wit: Elijah Hendrick. (P.96)

Baliss HOUSE - 1806 Will - Son Thomas House negroes. Son
John House negroes. Son George House, negroes. Son William House,
negroes. Son James House, negroes. Son Baliss House, negroes.
Appoints son Thomas House and John Gardner, executors. No date of
writing shown. Wit: John O. Mitchell, Willis C. Holland, Stephen
Norris. (P.98)

Jonathan LATIMER - November 13, 1802 Will - Wife Lucretia use
of property. Children: Hannah Latimer. Charles Latimer, my
blacksmith tools. Robert Latimer. Griswold to have my wagon.
Joseph. Grandsons, William and Nathan Latimer, lands on Red River.
Charles and Griswold Latimer are named as sons. (P.99)

John McGUIRE - September 14, 1803 Will - Wife to have household goods. Son George McGuire one-half of my plantation. Son
Thomas McGuire one-half of my plantation. Daughters Sally Bell,
Marion GILLESPIE, Sidney BRANDON, Agness RUTHERFORD and each of them
and their husbands. Appoints sons Thomas and George McGuire
executors. Witnesses: George Gillespie, Abel Brandon. (P.100)

Charles LARRENCE - December 8, 1806 Will - Children under age.
Wife and children (not called by name). Wife Betsy. My brothers
Robert and John Laurence. Wit: Thomas Campbell Sr. and Jr. (P.101)

William HENDERSON - November 28, 1806 Will - Wife Lucky land
purchased of William Hawkins. Children under age not named. Son
Arthur Mosesly Henderson. Son Daniel Littleton Henderson. Son
John C. Henderson land on Sanders fork of Smith's fork. Son Bennett
Hidson Henderson. Son William T. Henderson land in Wilson Co. on
Hickman Creek, Wilson County, Tenn. Son Bennett H. Henderson town
lots in Franklin. Son Lilbourn L. Henderson land on Wilkerins
(Wilkerins) Creek. Son Granville, land. Son Daniel L. and Arthur
Mosely 2 tracts of land. Daughters Pauline Ann, Elizabeth, Maria,
and Malinda (called Lickey Malinda) money and land in Kentucky.
Grandson Bennett Henderson son of John C. Henderson. Son Abram
Henderson. Executors Sons Bennet H., Daniel L., Henderson, and
Edward Sanders. Witnesses: Drury Milner, Stephen Pettus and
Isaac Clucke. Codicil Feb. 8, 1807. (P.102)

Robert HARRIS - August 14, 1806 Will - Wife. Son Robert
Harris, 1000 acres land near the Ohio. Daughter Agnes Cunringham
GOHEN, $20.00 cut of last bond due me in Virginia. If she die to
her grandson Harris Cohea. Daughter Agnes JORDEN. Daughter Mary
Gibson Harris. Money to wife due from Virginia. Daughter Frances
Houston ROBINSON an equal share of Virginia money. Daughter
Aranhita Juliet OBE all she now has and money from Virginia.
Daughter Sarah Caroline SIMPSON all she now has and money from
Virginia. Son Robert Brooks a Bible and land in Virginia.
Daughter Martha Spurr HARRIS money from Virginia. Daughter
Elizabeth Henrietta Harris money from Virginia. Thomas Leroy

12

Harris books (his relationship not stated). All children are not of age. Each child to have a bible with date of birth written in each. Son Blair Harris and Son-in-law Greenberry ORR as executors. Wit: Josiah E. Giles, Albert Holmes and John Giles. (P.105/6)

Richard TAYLOR - 1807 Will - Wife Charlotte during her widowhood. Sons Tilden and Richard Taylor land now live on. Son Richard Taylor, negroes. Daughter Charlotte, negroes. Daughter Amelia Taylor, negroes. Appoints George D. Blackmore and Zacheus Wilson, son of late Major David Wilson executor. Witness: John H. Bush, John Johnson and Solomon Ruuse. (P.110)

Abraham HASSELL - March 17, 1807 Will - Wife Christian Hassell, negroes. Children: My son, Daughter Jennett, Daughter Priscilla. Appoints John Mitchell, Richard Strother and Jesse Hassell executors. March 17, 1807. Witnesses: Edward Warrington (Worrington) and Asa Hassell. (P.112)

Abraham ROGERS - March 17, 1807 Will - Appoints Abraham Hassell, Samuel Rogers and Moore Stevenson as executors. Wife Tobitha land whereon I now live. Son Samuel 60 acres land. Son Briton 80 acres land. Son James 60 acres land. Six daughters: Elizabeth ROGERS, Lucretia ROGERS, Sally ROGERS, Nancy Rogers, Theany Rogers, Patsey Rogers, each $100.00 in property.

Will of Thomas PERRY, dec'd. - September 1807 Will - Wife Catharine Perry (?) use of plantation. Son John Perry at wife's death to have the plantation, etc. William Rainey McAdams (relationship not stated) negroes. My five granddaughters: Nancy SMITH, Celia THOMPSON, Betsy CARTWRIGHT, Polly POWELL, Sarah POWELL. Son George Perry and grandson Thomas POWELL and my five granddaughters named before to have negroes, etc. Appoints son George Perry executor with wife Catherine as executrix. Wit: Isaac Walton, Shadrack Nye. (P.115)

John TRICE - December 20, 1803 Will - John Trice of Robertson County, Tennessee. Wife Patsey and my children: Not all of age; Nancy WOOD wife of James WOOD, William Anderson Trice, Patsey Darby Trice, Dorothy Anderson Trice, Adagela Trice, Emlyan Trice, John Trice. My wife probably pregrant with child. Children to have money, negroes, and land: Wife executrix and Thomas Keefe (?) executor. (P.116)

William KING - December 20, 1818 Bond - Washington County, Virginia. William D. Neilson, John Doherty, witness. Said Dougherty (Doherty) now residing in Mississippi Territory, about 1,000 miles from this place. James King and William Trigg, executors. Dated Mch. 3, 1806. Col. James King, Samuel Glen, Jacob Baker, maybe others. (P.118)

Robert PATTON, Senr. - November 26, 1806 Will - Wife Margaret during her life property. Son Robert real estate if have tender regards for his mother. Daughter Mary, misc. property. Son David $50.00 and etc. Sons John, William, Mathew, Samuel, James and daughter Mary at decease of my wife. Son Robert executor. Witness: John Whitsett, James Wright, Shadrack Nye. (P.120)

13

Jacob ARCHER - _____ - Will - Son Jacob land in Hartford Co,
N.C. Wife Sarah to have H.H. goods and etc. Oldest son Josiah
$40.00. Second son Hezekiah to have $40.00. Probably other children
not called by name. No date shown. (P.121)

Matt BROWN - April 3, 1808 Will - Daughter Isabel to have
money. Daughter Mary to have money. Daughter Ruth to have money.
Son Jaison to have land. Son John to have land. Son David to have
land. Wife Ann the Ferry and 20 acres land on each side of River
and H.H. goods. Son Samuel land on north side Cumberland River.
Samuel to give to each of the daughters Ann HANNER, and Jennett a
cow and calf apiece. Grandson Matthew Brown son of Jaison Brown
to have money. Sons Jaison and John Brown to be executors. (P.122)

Ruth OZBROOK - April 11, 1809 Will - Appoints friend William
Grainger exec. Divides estate between her two children William W.
Ozbrook and Nancy Ozbrook. Wit: Edward Gwin, William Grainger
and John Bradley. (P.123/4)

Patrick HAMILTON - July 10, 1809 Will - Wants estate divided
as follows: To my daughter Esther's heirs. Daughter Sarah.
Daughter Mary. Daughter Margaret. Daughter Dorsy. Son John.
Son-in-law Joseph POWAN. Son-in-law James HART. These two sons-
in-law to be executors. Witnesses: Wm. L. Alexander, Thomas
Donoho. (P.124)

James CLACK - June 23, 1809 Will - Wife Mary. Children under
age and wants them educated. Son Wright Clack the plantation.
Brother David Clack and friend William C. Anderson executors. Does
not call children by name. Witnessed by: Andrew Blythe, Archer
Skippen (?) and Cbworth Ruyans (?). (P.125)

Moses CUMMINGS - October 21, 1809 Will - Wife Margaret
Cummings. Divides property at wife's death. John Cotton and
William Edwards Jr. executors. Wit: Asa Hassell, Jesse Hassell,
J. Cryer. (P.127)

William KENNEDY - _____ October 20, 1809 Will - Wife Prudence
Kennedy my plantation etc. Son Armstrong Kennedy, Son John Kennedy.
My honored mother Nary Armstrong during her natural life the cabin
and the two acres of land whereon she now lives. My children:
Armstrong, John, Margaret, Rebecca, William, Daniel, Elizabeth,
Evelina, Alexander, Rachel, Simpson and Eliza. My son Armstrong W.
Kennedy and John Penny executors. Wit: John Tinnon, Samuel
Tinnon, Edmonds Hogan, Shadrack Nye. (P.128)

William F. McNUTT - June 5, 1809 Will - To my sister Jane
McNutt personal property. To my brother James McNutt. To Nancy
FINDLEY daughter of CONNALLY FINDLEY of Abingdon, I give and
bequeath one eight part of my real and personal property. To my
brother Thomas McNutt. Thomas McNutt and Connally Findley of
Abingdon executors. Wit: James Barry, George King. (P.129)

14

George HUNT - November 12, 1807 Will - George Hunt of Halifax
County, Virginia. My son George Hunt. My son James Hunt. My
daughter Nelly ISBELL, and her two children, Patsy and Frances Isbell.
My daughter Nancy SIMPKINS. My wife Lucy Hunt. Sons George and James
executors. Wit: George Isbell, Martin McCarty and Mourning Isbell.
(P.130)

William PHIPPS - December 27, 1809 - Wife Mary. Son Joseph. Son
William. Daughter Polly Lane (?) (Love). Son-in-law Isaac Love (Lane)
Son-in-law James Lane. Daughter Sarah Lane. (P.132)

Thomas MARTIN - _____ - Will - Friend Daniel Smith to have land.
Wife Agnes Martin executor. (P.134)

Samuel CONN - July 31, 1810 Will - Sister Lydia TOMPKINS to have
house and lot whereon I now live. Sister Petavia Conn lot adjoining
the one I now live on, and notes on James White of Abingdon. My
nephew Joseph Gill 137 acres on Bledsoe Creek. My nephew James Gill
land on East fork of Bledsoe's Creek. Friend John Brown $100.00. My
brother Joseph H. Conn, exec. (P.134)

Ann GRIER - August 6, 1810 Will - Sons John Motheral, Son Samuel
Motheral. Son Joseph Motheral. Son James Grier. Mary Donelson to have
negroes. My daughter Jean JOHNSON. My daughter Mary DONALSON. My
daughter Margaret CAVIN. Witnesses: Sarah Motheral, Jane Motheral and
Thomas Donnell. (P.135)

Drury WALTON - 1810 Will - Mentions Mabry but does not say he is a
son, must be a son. Among children names Patsey ROE. Does not name his
children but mentions his children and his wife. Test: Andrew Allison,
Garland Tenney, William Exum. (P.137)

James REED - May 25, 1811 Will - Wife Hannah. Children: William,
Thomas, Agness, James, John, and Elizabeth. Sons Thomas and Wilson
Yandall executors. Witnesses: John Sloan, John Smothers, Sr., John
Smothers, Jr. (P.137)

Henry YOUNG - 1811 Will - Wife Mary. Children but does not name
them. Wife and Henry McAdin executors. Wit: Wilson Yandell, William
White and Isam Cooper. (P.138)

William CAGE - May 15, 1810 Will - Wife Elizabeth. Son Jesse
Cage. Son Reuben Cage. Daughter Betsey. Daughter Patsey. Son-in-law
Jack Carr. Son Lofton. Son Edward. Son-in-law William Hale. Son
Richmond. Son Albert. Sons Harry and Robert. Nancy Cage daughter of
Reuben Cage. Cyrus Hale son of William Hale. Son Loftain land on
Clinch River. (P.139)

Daniel MILTON - Apl. 8, 1811 Will - Wife Mary. Amy HOWARD.
Children: Polly READ, Patsey ROBINSON, Sealy Milton, Liney Milton and
Nancy HURPER (?). (P.141)

James CAROTHERS - _____ - Will - Wife Jean. Daughters Dorsy and
Polly. Daughter Peggy. Brother Hugh Carothers and my wife executors.
(P.143)

Martha FERRELL - June 14, 1810 Will - Son Burtin Fenel (Ferrel), negroes. William Douglas executor. Daughter Cloe Ferrel. Daughter Zadia Ferrell. Daughter Cheary Ferrel. My cousin Rebeccah Ferrel now living with me. My sons Alsa Ferrel, Asa HUNT and my daughter Nancy Ferrel, not to receive any part of estate. Witness: W. Douglass, David George, Fielding Grimsley. (P.147)

Ambrose TRUMBO - August 30, 1811 Will - Brother George my part of plantation where I now live which I purchased of my two brothers-in-law after his paying Jacob Trumbo's two daughters $150.00 each. Andrew Burns and Morgan Burns owes him. Orphas child now living with me. George Trumbo and Wm. Kirk executors. Wit: Henry Vinson, Robert Lawrence. (P.148)

Benjamine WILLIAMS - June 18, 1811 Will - Wife Mary. Children: My daughter Peggy. My son James. My son Allen. My daughter Betty. My daughter Molly. My daughter Pruely (Prudey). Wife and William Lambuth executors. Wit: James Roney, Sr., Jonathan Spooner; Jesse McCollister. (P.149)

Alexander YOUREE - February 20, 1810 Will - Wife Meary. (Mary) Son Wm. P. Youree. Son Francis Youree. Daughter Susannah HUTCHINS. My son Patrick Youree. My daughter Fanny RUTLEDGE. Wit: Francis Youree, Patrick Youree. James Bentley. (P.150)

Lawrence RICHARDSON - October 3, 1811 Will - Wife Margaret. Wit: Charles Locke, William Parr. (P.151)

William BOYLE (BOGLE ?) - 1811 Will - My wife Elizabeth PRACKEN Bogle. My friend William BRACKEN to be executor. Wit: Andrew Dinning, William Dinning (part of this will is gone). (P.152)

William COWDEN - November 11, 1811 Will - Wife Elizabeth. Four children, Amcy Cowden, Lockey Cowden, Lucy Cowden, and Susannah Cowden (when of age). Friend James Cowden and John Maacey (?) executors. William Cowden, Jr. Wit: John Selivent(?) probably intended for Sullivan), George Clabun, Josiah Cowden. (P.153)

Thomas PARKER - May 8, 1810 Will - Wife Judah Parker. My sons Grandeson and Coleman. My daughter Milly. My daughter Chloe. My daughter Rhoda. My daughter Anney. Wife and Larkin Jackson executors. Wit: Thomas Donoho, John Jones, Goleman Donoho. (P.154)

Robert LATIMER - January 26, 1812 Will - Wife Lucinda. Son Hugh. Son Burastus. Sons Benjamine A., Robert. My daughter Betsy. Daughter Nancy HITCHELL. Daughter Fanny HAMBLETON. Son Hugh and wife executors. Wit: Benjamine Hudson. Joshua Williams, Elizabeth Williams. (P.155)

Isaac LINDSEY Jr. - February 13, 1812 - Will - Son Isaac who is traveling. Children, Sally, Peggy, and Ruth. Ezekiel. My son-in-law Lewis CRAIN 88 acres land where Milleton Walls formerly

16

lived adjoining Abraham Ellis. My son-in-law John Pearcy 140 acres on Hurricane Creek of Stones River. My daughter Prudence 110 acres adjoining John Pearcy. My daughter Peggy land adjoining Ellis. My daughter Sally 114 acres land on Bledsoe's Lick and Spencers Creek, including Barrows Cabbins. My daughter Ruth 88 acres including place where Abraham Ellis now lives. Mentions Prudence ELLIS and her husband Abraham Ellis. Son and Lewis Crain executors. Wit: Samuel Haw, Mary Baker and Patsy Baker. (P.157)

Nathaniel PARKER, Jr - February 25, 1811 Will - My son Robert land adjoining Hugh Rogans, David Shelbys and Isaac Parkers line. Sons, John, Thomas, Richard, Isaac, Nathaniel, and Robert. My daughter Betsey COLGER. My daughter Mary THOMPSON. My second wife's daughter Nancy Parker. Sons Thomas and Isaac Parker to be executors. Wit: Hugh Rogan. (P.162)

James C. ALDERSON - October 27, 1810 Will - Court held at Kingston Roane Co, Tenn., April 1811. James C. Alderson's will proved. Jared Hotihkiss and H.K. Hotchkiss witnessed. Will recites that Alderson was of Sumner Co. Wife. My youngest daughter Jeney STEPHENSON when she arrives to the age of 6 years. One of my eldest daughters Sarah or Nancy. Children: Sarah, Nancy, Betty, Daniel, Mary and Jeney Stephenson. John Polk and my wife Jane executors. (P.162)

William SNODDY Senr. - April 13, 1812 Will - Daughter Rebeckah PORTER. Daughter Peggy COOPER. Daughter Elizabeth Snoddy. Son David Snoddy. Son William Snoddy. Son Adam Snoddy. Youngest sons Graham and Adam. Daughter Sarah Snoddy. Youngest sons Samuel Panard and son David Snoddy executors. Wit: Wm. Snoddy, Thomas Wilson. (P.164)

Absalum CLOAR- March 1, 1813 Will - Wife Anne. Son William (when he arrives of age 21 years). Wife now pregrant. John Hubert, executor. Wit: Henry Head, Overton Harris, John Harris. (P.165)

Basil TRAIL - December 7, 1812 Will - Son Solomon Trail. Daughter Sally MOOR. Son David Trail. Daughter Elizabeth SMITH. Son John. Son Hamelton. Wife Elizabeth. Henry Belote and Jesse Scean executors. Wit: Jacob Bearnard, David Bernard, Peter Archeron (Atcherson), John Herlon, James Williams. (P.167)

Richard STROTHER - September 23, 1809 Will - Sumner Co, Tenn. Wife Susannah. Son James. Son Robert. Daughter Susanna PITT land I bought of David Briggance she now lives on. My 5 children: Nancy HOLLIS, James Strother, Robert Strother, Betsy McCONNELL and Susanna PITT. Son James and John McConnell as executors. Wit: James Cryer, John Cotton, James Reed. (P.168)

David KING - December 23, 1813 Will - Sister Rebecka King. Sister Elizabeth King certain land. Bledsoe's Lick. Wit: Richard King, Miles McCorkle. (P.169)

John COOPER - May 10, 1813 Will - John Cooper. Daughter Mary MADES. Daughter Rachel MORTON. Daughter Franke. Daughter Purify. Son John. Property to be divided between Nancy, Bathsheba, Hannah,

17

Betsy, Franke, Purify and John. Son John executor. Wit: George
Cooper, Jesse Weaver. (P.170)

John SLOSS - April 3, 1813 Will - Wife Jane. Daughter Sarah
Sloss land in Warren Co, Kentucky. Friend Joseph Motheral and
Joseph Sloss executors. Wit: Thomas Donnell, Joseph Robert and
Elizabeth Motheral. (P.171)

Lunsford PITTS - June 26, 1813 Will - Son Burton H., Son
Henry, Son Lunsford C. Children of son Burton namely, Lunsford,
George Gaines, and Rebecca Pitts. Mentions having paid Henry
Fetherson Sr. My daughter Lucy FETHERSTON, My daughter Fanny
BLACK. My daughter Betsy YANDALL. My daughter Judith YANDALL.
My grandson Lunsford Pitts YANDELL. Samuel P. Black, Charles
Fetherston, Wilson Yandell, and John Yandell as executors. Wit:
M.D.S.F. Sharp and Wm. Craven. Samuel Wootton. (P.172)

A(K)intuckey MESSER (MERCER) - August 11, 1813 Will - Sister
Nelly GRAHAM as executor. Wit: George Gillespie, John Layne. (P.175)

Henry RUYLE - February 16, 1790 Will - Wife Catherine. My
eldest son Henry. Son Andrew. Son John. Son Solomon. Son Moses.
Son Aaron. Son Peter. Daughter Mary CRAVENS. Daughter Magdalin
JONES. Daughter Margarett. Daughter Elizabeth. Daughter Celia
COTES. Wife Catherine and son John executors. Witnesses: A.
Philips, John Cravens, Edward Jones. (P.176)

L.A.BRADFORD - September 27, 1813 Grant - L.A.Bradford grants
Elizabeth Baker (daughter of Isaac Baker) all my property. If I
return well from an expedition now on foot to the Creek Nation of
Indians the above be voyed and of no effect. (P.177)

Jain CORETHERS - October 7, 1813, Pvd. 1814 Will - My
daughter Dovey. Daughter Polley. Hugh Corothers and Jonathan
Wilson executors. Witnesses Zanus Wilson, William Ball. (P.178)

John KEY - August 26, 1811 Will - John Key of Albemarle Co,
Virginia. Daughter Polley Bibb FLADES. Mentions John C. BLAIDES.
Son Strother Key. Son John Key. Son Richard Key. Son Winn Key.
Son Jesse Bibb Key. Wit: Jesse Bibb Key and John Watron
(Watson) executors. (P.179)

James HOLLIS - March 26, 1814 Will - Wife Margaret. Son
James Morgin Hollis. My daughter Ann Hollis. My four children,
namely, Jesse, James Morgan, Ann Hollis, and Elizabeth MARTIN.
Wit: Jesse Hollis and Edward Wormington executors. Wit: Edwd.
Wormington, William King, John Donohoe. (P.181)

John STARK - April 5, 1814 Will - Son Thornton Stark negro
which I bought of Mr. Bailey Washington in Virginia. Son John
Stark. Wife Sarah Stark. Daughter Prudence Stark. Daughter
Charlotte. Daughter Elizabeth SHELTON. Daughter Tarver BYRAM.
Son Jeremiah Stark. Son Alexander. My grandson John son of Alexander
Stark. Wife Sarah. Wit: Daniel Smith, Thomas Stark.

18

John D. HANNA - March 31, 1814, Pvd. 1814 Will - Wife. Two sons Richard Hall under 21 years of age and Robert Hanner. Daughter Agness. William Hall Hanna executor. Wit: Benj. Rawlings, John Rawlings, Edward Rawlings. (P.183)

Thomas SWANN - 27 ___ 1814, Pvd. May 1814 Will - Now in the City of Natchez and Mississippi Territory. Wife Emelia C. now residing at Cairo in State of Tenn. Mentions lands in Jackson Co, Tenn. Wife to have negro girl now in State of Virginia. Wife as executor. Wit: John Gordon, Benj. P. Howard, Joseph Baxter, Stephen Trigg. (P.184)

Nathan Holloway, witness to statement of Thomas TAYLOR - November 7, 1813 - Condition Will - Now at Camp Fort Strother. Nathan Holloway swore that he was called upon by Thomas Taylor, deceased, who was then a soldier with him to take notice that should he be killed and I not for me to see that his Brother John Taylor's son Bledsoe receive his property. (P.186)

William DOUGLASS - 18 ___? Proved 1814 Will - Wife Margaret. Son Alfred Douglass. Property to be divided between John Douglass, Elizabeth SEOBY, Aldred W. Douglass, Jesse Douglas, illegetimate son of Elizabeth Seoby, Polly DIMENT, Alexander Howell an illegetimate ___?, and Sally MAYS deceased ___?. Alfred Douglas my son executor. (Record torn and lost.) Wit: John Watson Senr., Anderson Stroud. (P187)

Henry BARNES - December 3, 1813 Nuncupative Will - Henry Barnes a private in Capt. John W. Pyrn's Co. gives Henry Fletcher son of John Cotton of Sumner Co. all property in case I should fall during the campaign against Creek Indians. Dec. 8, 1813. Wit: George S. Brigance, Elisha Stallions. (P.188)

George LOGAN - September 16, 1814, Proved November 1814 Will - Wife Hester (record lost) (record partly lost). Alexander. Daughter Peggy Alexander and Morish. Daughter Emaline (when she arrives at the age of 18 yrs). It would appear from the reading that all the children are under age. Wit: James Adams, Ferisha Turner, Lewis Graham. (P.189)

Thomas GRAVES (name not clear - GROVES) - September 1814, pvd. 1814 Will - Thomas Graves (will partly lost and torn). Wife Eady. John Graves. Son Thomas 200 acres where he now lives. Allen Graves. Daughter Gilley GRAINGER and her children. (not by name). My daughter Betsy. Daughter Rhoda. My daughter ___? . My daughter ___. Son Isaac. Daughter Leah. Son Davis. Thomas and Allen Graves my sons executors. Wit: J. W. Harris, William Roney, Gilley Grainger. (P.191)

William EDWARDS - October 18, 1814, pvd. November 1814 Will - William Edwards will. Wife Maria. Son James. Mentions lands conveyed by William W. Waters in the Territory of Missouri upper Louisiana Territory at Cape Geraudiau. My daughter Mary CRENSHAW. Sons Edward, David, and my Son-in-law WILLIAM OWEN. Wit: Willis Aunley, Willie Bohannan, Andrew Graham. (P.192)

James SMOTHERS - August 25, 1814 Will - Wife Mary. Aunt Jemima Summers. Wit: Jacob Harden, Levi Summers. Exec. Wm. David, Esqr. Margaret Smothers, and Thomas Smothers. (P.194)

John BOREN - 1814 Will - (partly gone) Wife Sarah Boren. Daughter Margaret. Daughter Rebyckah... Rest of my children not called by name. Wit: Mathew Boren, Wm. Melton, and W. Boren. (P.195)

John B. GILLAM - August 12, 1811 Will - John B. Gillam of Smith County Tenn., states he is moving. Wife Jane. Mentions property in possession of his mother in Campbell Co, Virginia, to his brother Janet (or James) Gillam. Wit: Wm. Turnbul, Samuel Anthony. (P.196)

Peggy CAROTHERS - April 21, 1814, Pvd. 1814 Will - Peggy Carothers by Daniel J. Greene. Brother Ezekiel Carothers. To Frankey Patton (relation not stated). Wit: Daniel J. Greene, David Wilson, John Goodman. (P.197)

William CAROTHERS - September 18, 1814, Pvd. 1814 Will - By Daniel Greene (part of will lost). Ezekiel Carothers. Sister Sally. My son James and Polly Scot. David Wilson executor. Wit: Hugh Carothers, James Scott. (P.198)

Samuel WILSON - April 9, 1814, Pvd. February 1815 Will - (will partly gone) Wife Sarah. Son John, son James. Elizabeth Wilson's family. Wife to live with son James. Grandson Samuel Wilson son of John Wilson land on Duck River the Rattle Snake Spring. Zacheus Wilson deceased. Jonathan Wilson executor. Wit: Wm. Bell, Willis Hall. (P.199)

David PEARD Senr. - January 6, 1815, Pvd. February 1815 Will - (partly gone) Youngest son Thomas. My daughter and my three daughters-in-law the wives of my sons Adam, David, and Samuel. David Peard and Thomas Carson Peard executors. Witnesses: Carson Dobbins, Elizabeth Dobbins. (P.200)

Norman PEEK - December 23, 1814, Pvd. 1815 Will - (partly gone) Wife Ann. Joshua Smith and Silas Fulghum land where on the widow Grainger formerly lived. Wife executor. James McKendree and Joshua Smith. Nephew Juffry Peek and nephew Jessey Peek sons of William and Eason Peek, and Nathaniel Simmons (Simmons) son of John and Elizabeth Simmens. Mentions Jeffrey Smith. Wit: Joseph G. Morris, Leonard Ferrell, Nicholas Overby, Henderson Parnal. (P.201)

Abraham BLEDSOE - March 5, 1815, Pvd. May 1815 Will - (will partly gone) Wife Milley Bledsoe. My two oldest daughters Mariah and Sealy. Eldest son David S. Bledsoe. My son James. My daughter Polly. Wit: Geo Gillespie, J.T. Humphrey, James Wallace. (P.202)

Stephen WINCHESTER - April 12, 1815, Proved May 1815 Will - (partly gone) David Winchester. Joshua Howard. My children to receive an education. Appoints my brother General James Winchester and my two friends George Roberts and A.B. Shelby executors. Wit: A.C. Gillespie, Mr. P. Winchester. (P.204)

Andrew HAMELTON - March 14, 1815, pvd. August 1815 Will - (will is partly gone) Land myself and James HART purchased of Thomas Harris on Round Lick Creek. My deceased sisters Esther & Margaret. My sister Sarah. My sister Mary. My nephew William Rowan. My brother John W. Hamelton. John son of Patrick Hamelton (under age). John W. Hamelton. William L. Alexander executors. Wit: Rd. Alexander, Ethelbert Sanders, Polly M. Cunningham. (P.205)

John P. JOHNSON - February 12, 1815, pvd. August 1815 Will - (partly gone) My brother Chapman Johnson. Wife Elizabeth. My children until my second son Chapman arrives at the age 10 years old the 21st Oct. last comes of age. My three children Thomas, Chapman and Mariah. Executor to be wife Elizabeth and my brother Chapman Johnson of the State of Virginia. Wit: W. Hunt, William Bloodworth, Mark C. Hollisson. (P.206)

John HARGROVE - October 1, 1815, pvd. November 1815 Will - (partly) gone) Polly Hargrove daughter of my brother William Hargrove of North Carolina, negroes. To my other neice Nancy Hargrove the 2nd daughter of my brother William of North Carolina. Nancy Hargrove, Anna Hargrove. My Neice Polly _____ daughter of my sister Anna Hargrove ___?__ . To Doakes Prewitt of ___?__ . My neighbor _____ son. George Smith. My sister Anna Hargrove and her two daughters Nancy and Polly Hargrove. Sally Singleton. Appoints friend Thomas Preston executor. Wit: Daniel Smith, William Pittman, Thomas Preston. (P.207)

Thomas DUGGER - July 27, 1815 Will - (partly gone) Wife Charlotte. My son Thomas. Mentions negroes in Virginia and land where my mother dies. Thomas Featherston now an infant (under age to be reared). Sterling Orgain and Hubbard Sanders executors. Wit: Alexander Stark, Lucy Sims, Milly Carrell. Elizabeth Carrell. (P.208)

Mary Ann GARDNER - June 26, 1812, pvd. 1815 Will - (partly gone) My granddaughter Mary Ann SLOAN. To Mary Ann KELOUGH (KILLOUGH). To Margaret KELOUGH. My granddaughter Mary Ann GILES. Ann Bradley. My daughter Mary. My daughter ___?__ HARRIS. Rachel Harris. Abby Clark. Rachel Morris. Abigail Clark. Jean Read. Eliza Pradley. John Barr and John Sloan executors. Wit: John Barr, Margaret Barr, Polly Barr. (P.209)

Samuel BUGG - February 3, 1816, Proved 1816 Will - (partly gone) Wife Frances Bugg. Land I purchased from Wm. Avent. Sons, Anselem Bugg, Henry Willis Bugg, John Langley Bugg, Samuel Howel Bugg, Walter Lewis Bugg. My daughter Ann Bugg. My daughter Joyce Bugg. My daughter Mary Ann Bugg. (P.210)

Joseph MOTHEREL (MOTHERAL) - October 23, 1815, Pvd. 1816 Will - (part of will gone) Wife. Daughter Jain (Jane) land I bought of Robert Cartwright. Daughter Polly land whereon I live. Children: Anny ROBB, Jain SLOSS, Betsy GLOVER, Polly Motherel. Joseph Robb and Wm. Glover, executors. Wit: Adlai Donnell, Thomas Donnel, William Bennett, Albert Hodge. (P.213)

Joseph BARRON (could be BARROW as there was a BARROW family in the Co.) - November 5, 1815 Will - (partly gone) Two daughters Mary P. Barron and Jane Parron. My sister-in-law Margaret Glover. My sister Jane Therborn (who I expect lives in County Antrim in Ireland). Catherine Hillays (Hilbays) son. Son Gale Barron my plantation in Anderson Co, Tenn. To Catharine HELFAY's daughter Joanna Barron my house and lot in Williamsburgh, Jackson Co, Tenn. My brother-in-law Mr. Dabney FINLEY of Kentucky executor. Wit: James Barry, Ashley Standfield, George Crocket. (P.213)

Lydia TOMPKINS - February 13, 1816, Pvd. February 1816 Will - (partly gone) My sister Ann Burton. My brother Jeffhus H. Conn. To Lydia Eliza Prown daughter of John Prown. My neice Lydia Purton. My brother-in-law John Prown to be executor. Wit: Jno. Shelby, Stephen R. Roberts. (P.214)

James BUSBY - January 29, 1816, proved February 1816 Will - (part of will gone) My daughter _____. My wife Dou _?_ . My children, My first born Polly Busby, Andrew Busby, Levy Busby, Henry Busby, Betsy Busby, Ann Busby, Patsy Busby, Susannah Busby, Howard Busby, Dorethe Busby. My brothers Wm. Busby and Stephen Busby executors. Wit: John Cotton, John Mitchell, James Prigance. (P.215)

Enos BENTHALL - March 24, 1816, Rec. May 1816 Will - (partly gone) Mother Mary Lassater. Bros. Willis Benthall, Daniel Penthall, Laban Benthall. Capt. James Vinson executor. Wit: Enos Vinson and James Hamelton. (P.216)

William MARTIN - December 29, 1815, Pvd. May 1816 Will - (partly gone) My son Olliver Martin. Martha ____. My son ____ Martin. My children viz: William, Rachel, Danal, Frederick, Jemminy, Ollaver, Luis and Sarah. Wit: Edward Given Sr., Samuel Roney, Edward Gwin, Jr. (the name Given may have been Gwin) (P.218)

Robert BOYKIN - May 1816 Will - (partly gone) Wife Delilah Boykin. Wit: James Boykin. John Blayingame. Damiel Webb. (P.223)

Elisha THOMAS - March 27, 1816 Will - (partly gone) Wife. Son Robert and wife executors. Son Wm. Thomas and my daughter _____. Robert Thomas. Washington Thomas (Tomas). Elizabeth. Eliza. Wit: Wm. Crenshaw. Ro T. Brown. (P.225)

Nathan RICKMAN - April 20, 1816 Will - (partly gone) Wife Franky to keep the plantation I now live on. My children. not called by name. Son Thomas. Youngest sons David H. and ____ and John S. and Mark Rickman. Children under age. Son Thomas executor with wife. Wit: Benja. Seawell. Isaac Leath, Samuel Henry. (P.226)

John BRIGANCE - February 21, 1816, Pvd. May 1816 Will - Wife Patsy. Children, Mahala, Stuart, Plantain, Joel Dyer. John Stuart, William Henry and Alexander Brigance. Henry R. Willis and George S. Brigance, and David Berrot. (P.228)

22

William CRAIN - April 14, 1816, pvd. May 1816 Verbal Will - of
William Crain. De died April 14, 1816. Wife Susannah. Her father
Lewis Crain. My three sons of John Crain, Lewis W. Crain and Isaac
Crain tend my plantation. The will communicated to writing April 20,
1816. Wit: Lewis Crain. (P.228)

James EASLEY - March 15, 1814, Pvd. May 1816 Will - Wife. My
six children. My six youngest children names not mentioned. James
Hunt and John Hunt were witnesses. (P.229)

John BADGETT - April 5, 1816 Will - Jane and Elizabeth Badgett.
My children. My son John. My wife Nancy. Polly MOORE, Tabitha HAIL,
Jane Badgett, all my living children. Also Elizabeth Padgett and John
Badgett my living children. Wit: Lewis Johnson, Thomas Badgett,
John A. Hail. (P.229)

Nathaniel S. ANDERSON - May 22, 1816, proved May 1816 Will -
Nathaniel S. Anderson of Nashville, Tenn. will. Speaks of his negro
girl at Shewnee Town, in Illinois. Brother Turner W. Anderson my
house and lease whereon it stands in Nashville. My brother John D.
Anderson 15 shares in Nashville Bank. My sister Mary FLEMING 25
share in Nashville Bank. Gilbert G. Washington and my brother John D.
Anderson executors. Wit: A.R.Shelby, Robert Desha, Jr. (P.230)

James HASTEN, James HARTEN (poor script) - March 6, 1816, proved
May 1816 - Will - Wife Jenny Harten. Sons Thomas Harten and William
Harten. Sons Joseph, Nathaniel and Archibald Harten. The last two
under age of 18 years. Daughters Peggy Harten and Mary Harten. Son
John executor. (P.231)

Wm. PURVIS - April 1, 1816, pvd. May 1816 Will - Wife Sally
Purvis. Her children. Harty, Harmer and Hetty. My three children,
Henry Purvis, Sally Purvis, and Wm. Purvis. My son James Purvis. My
son Edward Purvis. My son John Purvis. Wit: David Allen. Kichen
Carter. (NOTE: Her three children were probably named Harty, Harmer,
and Hetty Pigg. No proof but there is indication) (note by Whitley)
(P.231)

Elijah HUMPHREYS - August 6, 1816, proved August 1816 Will -
Nephew Charles L. Humphreys 220 acres coming to me from Thomas Murrey.
Relative Sally Humphreys daughter of my neice Caty Humphreys, land.
Nephew David Humphreys land. My sister Rachel Humphreys. My brother
Dr. Solomon Humphreys. My nephew Elijah Humphreys. Nephew Charles L.
Humphreys executor. Wit: W. Hall, W.M.Kerr. Isaac Lane. (P.232)

Robert DESHA - May 6, 1816, proved 1816 Will - Son John Desha
$1,000.00. Son Joseph $100.00. Son James. Daughter Nancy KILLGORE
$100. etc. Grandson John Drummond until the decease of his mother Nancy
Killgore. My daughter Nelly COCKE. Sons Robert and Benjamine. Daughter
Polly RUSE (REESE). Her husband Chas. Reese. Some of children under age.
Sons Robert and Benjamine. Daughter Betsy DOWELL and her children
(her husband Benj. DOWELL). My grandson Israel Reese (Ruse). My land
in Louisiana Territory and Mississippi. Son Robert and James Winchester
executors. (P.235)

Martha ALVIS - March 21, 1816 'Will - Sons Ashley and Elijah, Daughter Nancy. Son Ashley and Nancy executors. Wit: Hugh B. Stephenson. John H. Stephenson. (P.238)

William H. HINSON - November 16, 1816, Pvd. November 1816 Will - Wife Elizabeth. My son Josiah Hinson. John and Thomas Hinson executors. Wit: John Hinson, Thomas Hinson.(P.242)

Richard HALL - December 31, 1816, Pvd. February 1817 Will - Richard Hall. Wife Elizabeth. Mentions money owing in South Carolina. My granddaughter Betsy POULDING. My granddaughter Celia HALL. My grandson Glover Hall. My grandson Clement Hall. My grandson Neal Hall. Jemimah Hall wife of my son Wm. Hall deceased. Nephew General William Hall, of Sumner Co. Four grandsons Richard Hall, Redding Hall, Carter Hall, and Jesse Hall. Witness: David Humphreys, C.S.Humphreys. (P.243)

Peter LEMMONS, Sr. - October 28, 1816, Pvd. February 1817 Will - Of Giles County, Tenn. John Lemmons, William Lemmons, Arthur Hicks executors. Wife Mary. Children: Martha HAFFEINGTON, oldest daughter Lundy, John Lemmons, William Lemmons, Mary HICKS, and Peter Lemmons Jr. Grandson Isaac HUFFINGTON (under age). Wit: Joseph Spradling, Stephen Tuble. (P.245)

William GILLESPIE - February 22, 1816, Proved February 1817 Will - Daughter Polly. Son Jack. Daughter Sophia. Daughter Nancy. Son James. Son Robert. My children: Sons Barry and Allen, Betsy, Sally Elmiron, and Patsy (under age). Daughter Sophia under age. Wit: Enos Lassetar. (P.247)

Alexander ROBERTSON - February 15, 1816, Proved March 13, 1816. 1817 Will - Alexander Robertson's will. Allows Nancy McDonall privilege of my house and lot and when my child by her by name of Polly arrives at age. (P.250)

West EDWARDS - February 5, 1815, Pvd. 1815 Will - Wife Elizabeth. Her children: Sally Edwards and Polly Ann Whitfield Edwards. Under age. Children: Thomas Fitzhugh Edwards, John Jones Edwards, Nancy West Edwards, Drewry Edwards, Miles Edwards, Elizabeth Fitzhugh, Sally Edwards, Daughter Polly Ann Whitfield Edwards. Wife and two sons Thomas and John executors. Wit: Thomas Price, James Ruff. Proved May 1815 Green Co, N.C. (P.258)

Leonard DUGGER - Will - Family to move to Illinois. to Madison County, on waters Sliver Creek. Has land there. Wife Elizabeth $100. Son Jon $100. Youngest daughter Nancy $100. Dau. Elizabeth Hunter (Henter) equal part. Six children James, Westley, Polly, Elizabeth, John and Nancy. Family Bible to wife; Books to children. Wife and son John and 2 daughters live together. Appoints wife Elizabeth and Jordan Uzzell, exec. Wit: Hugh Kirkpatrick, James Kirkpatrick, David Carthon. 25 Sept. 1817, Proved Nov. 1817. (P.256)

Will of William P. YOURIE - November 1817 - Son Alexander 160 acres in Sumner County, Cumberland River. Daughter Mary

24

Younree have the Robertson place at death of her mother, also at death
of her grandmother. Wife Nancy. My brother Francis Yourie's son Wm.
C. Yourie. My brother Patrick Yourie's daughter Fanny. My Brother
John Hutchen's son Wm. Yourie. Daughter Mary. Son Alexander and friend
Francis Yourie and my wife Nancy executors. No date. Codicil dated
Nov. 12, 1817, Proved Nov. 1817. (P.258)

William TRIGGS will - September 5, 1817, proved November 1817 -
Son Hardin Trigg. Property in Bedford Co, Va. Bonds to Trigg and
Rhodes executed in Bedford Co, Va. One third tract land I hold an
obligation on General James Robertson. One third of 640 acres to be
divided between Col. William Henderson's heirs my son and myself.
Son Alanson Trigg, land I live on, 420 acres I bought of Wm. Alexander
on Stones River. Amount due me on books in State of Virginia. Son's
mother living. Son Will 302 acres I live on. Son Daniel what I have
given him and Son Daniel what I have given him and amount on books in
Virginia. Son Abram what has been given him. Dau. Betsy Davis already
given (Robert Davis). Dau. Polly Quarles (married Roger Quarles). Dau.
Locky Sanders (md. Edward Sanders), 320 acres. Dau. Sarah Prown (md.
Bedford Brown) $600, land Mulherrin Creek. Daughter Nancy Hodge 640
acres (md. Samuel Hodge) land in Wilson Co, Tenn. Dau. Dosha Blythe
(md. Samuel K. Blythe).Grandmother Lett. (grandmother of children).
Sons Will and A. Trigg. Wife Sarah plantation I now live on. Appoints
Alanson, Will, Abram Trigg, Edward Sanders and Samuel K. Blythe as
executors. Wit: Thomas Preston, Wm. T. Henderson. (P.260)

Will of Abner BALL - Sick. Wife Polly F. Ball. Two children
Young Ball and Eliza Ball. Appoints Brother James and Brother Isaac
Exec. Nov. 26, 1817. Proved Feb. 1818. Witnesses: John Sloan,
John Stowens, Isaac Ball. (P.266)

Will of Daniel SMITH - Dated July 22, 1816, Proved October 19,
1817. Exec. James Sanders. Was a long will - Daughter Mary Sanders
upper part tract I live on. About 1280 acres. and 651 acres in Wilson
Co, Tenn, including Traugh Spring and plantation whereon Elisha Taylor
now lives. etc. Son George what I have given him. To Geo. Smith heirs
tract land 640 acres whereon James Whitworth has resided and 150 acres
part lower tract Briery Spring. Son George Smith. 130 acres. bought
of James Sanders. adjoining Col. Trigg and land Wilson Co. including
Leakes Lick. I bought of Richard Estis. 6501 acres. All land I
have in Kentucky. Wife Sally land. Was very wealthy man. (also see
another place) (P.267)

Robert ELLACE (ELLIS) - Will - Verbal will. 25 Aug. 1818. Wife
Diannah. Aug. 27, 1818. No children named. (P.273)

Peter WYNN - Will - Wife Elizabeth. Two nephews Henry Winn,
Elliott and John Fagan Elliott. Nieces Betsy Winn Elliott. Exec. my
wife and my brother-in-law James Elliott. Nov. 11, 1818. Proved Nov.
1818. Witnessed by James Wright, John Allen. (P.274)

Will of Jonathan WHITE - Wife Polly. Children. Nathan White,
John White, Sally White, Votion White, Julia White, Robert White,
William White, James White, Daughter Sally, Daughter Julia (both daus.
under age). Wife Polly exec. Sons Nathan and John joint exec. and joint

25

exec. and joint guardian to children. 10 Oct. 1818. Proved Nov. 1818. Witnesses: Wm. C. Courson, Rowland Hordy (Hardy). Abram McGehee and Theodorich Burton. (P.274-275)

Griffith DICKERSON - Will - Wife Matilda Dickerson. Nephew Griffith Dickerson son of Wyllie Dickerson. Appoints wife Matilda exec. and Bro Wyllie. Aug. 31, 1818. Witnesses: Samuel Gibson, James Neely, Reuben Bruce. Proved. (P.276)

Will of Abner BALL (recorded twice) - Wife Polly F. Ball, and my two children Young Ball and Eliza Ball. Appoints my two brothers, James Ball and Isaac Ball executors. 26 Nov. 1817. Witnesses: John Sloan, John Stowens, Isaac Ball. Proved Feb. 1818 (P.259 (266)

Will of Daniel SMITH (see another place - several pages duplicated in records) - Daughter Mary Sanders upper part of tract of land I live on. about 1280 acres and tract of 650 acres land Wilson County, including Traugh Spring (?) and plantation whereon Elisha Taylor now lives. Also 650 acres land and negroes Son George tract land 640 acres whereon James Whitworth has resided, also 150 acres part of which called lower tract including Briney Spring and house. Also tract land 130 acres I bought of James Sanders and which Col. Trigg lives adjoining to. Also rest of land in Wilson County about 740 acres including Leakes Lick and 100 acre tract I bought of Richard Estis. All land I have in Kentucky I will to be sold, divided money. My son George tract land 268 acres I bought of Thomas Masten, after Mrs. Masten's decease who is to have life estate in same. My wife Sally lower part of tract I live on about 1510 acres and other property. A riding carriage. Executors Wife and son George. 22 July 1816. Signed Dave Smith. Postscript. Oct. 19, 1817. Appoints James Sanders executor. Mentions land on Drake Creek. Mentions son of daughter Mary by name Daniel Donelson. And this is in belief her son Andrew J. Donelson will become sole owner of tract land on South side Cumberland River adjoining General Jackson and ____ Donelson. If Daniel Donelson become a part owner with his brother Andrew then the latter is to become equal including the Drake Creek land. Proved Aug. 1818. (P.267)

Verbal will of Robert ELLACE (ELLIS) - 25 Aug. 1818. The old woman meaning his wife Dinnah Ellace to have all property. Aug 27, 1818 (P.273)

Will of Peter WINN (recorded twice) - Wife Elizabeth to have her life all and at her death my land to be equally divided between two nephews Henry Winn Elliott and John Fagan Elliott. My niece Betsy Winn Elliott at decease of my wife Elizabeth, to have all negroes. Appoints wife Elizabeth executor and my brother-in-law James Elliott. 11 Nov. 1818. Proved Nov. 1818. (P.273)

Will of Jonathan WHITE - Wife Polly her life full power, at her death or marriage estate to be divided equally. My children

Nathan White, John White, Sally White, Vition White, Julia White,
William White, Robert White, James White. My daughter Sally and
daughter Julia not yet of age. Wife Polly executor. Oct. 10, 1818
(P.274)

Will of Jonathan WHITE, deceased - Proved by Rowland Horsly
and Abram McGeher (McGehee). (P.276)

Will of George GILLESPIE - Dated 15 June 1818, Proved Nov.
1818 - Wife Mary all property she had when I married her. Allow her
to live on my land near Franklin Town, part of that land whereon my
son George Gillespie now liveth whereon I ordered a house built for her
use. House of convenience & size with single roof; hued logs, under
and upon floors, laid brick or stone chimney on the land by Mr. Jones,
for my wife. Son John Gillespie that part of my land I now liveth on.
Son Thomas Gillespie 500 acres land hereon he formerly lived. My son
Jacob, plantation where on I live and that place lately intended
joining on west to John Graham. Daughter Molly Byrns what she has got
and $100.00. Daughter Nancy a case of drawers. Daughter Lydia. My
grandchildren children of my son Richard G. Gillespie, to B___ F.
Gillespie $300. To Lydia and Mary Gillespie $300.00. $300. to Lydia
and Mary Gillespie $300.00. My son George tract land land where he
lives now. My daughter Jenny Brison and her son George. My grandson
James Gillespie set blacksmith tools. Sons John and Jacob. My niece
Nelly Graham. Rest divided equally between John and Thomas Gillespie,
Molly Byrns, Jacob Gillespie and George Gillespie, and Nancy Bledsoe
and Jenny Brison. Mentions George Gillespie and Geo. Gillespie son
of John and Thomas Gillespie. Appts. sons John & Jacob Gillespie exec.
(P.278)

Will of Griffith DICKERSON - Wife Matilda all property. My
nephew Griffith Dickerson son of Wyllie Dickerson. Appoints wife
executor. My brother Wyllie Dickerson executor. Aug. 31, 1818.
Witnessed by Samuel Gibson. James Neely, Reuben Bruce. Proved.(P.276)

Will of Thomas CURRY - Wife Catharine Curry real and personal
property her life or widowhood. Divided between my children namely.
?   John Curry, Mary Curry, William Curry, Jane Curry, Benjamine
Curry, James Curry and Nancy Curry. Appoints wife and William Curry and
John Wallace executors. 27 October 1818. Proved Nov. 1818. (P.281)

Will of George ESPEY - 7 Aug. 1818. Wife Lucretia Espey, to have
one half of tract land I now live on, etc. Child or children she is now
pregnant with other half of land. Property. Appoints Henry Head
executor. Proved Nov. 1818. Wit: Pascal Head, David Brown. (P.282)

Thomas PRESTON - Will - August 13, 1818 - Property to wife and to
school children (not by name). Children not of age. Wife executrix.
My son William B. Preston additional property to him. The above was
written by James Sanders at request of Thomas Preston. 13 Aug. 1818.
Proved Nov. 1818. (P.284)

Robert ELLACE (ELLISS) will - Verbal will. 25 Aug. 1818. On his
death bed. Wanted his "old woman" Dinna Ellace, his wife to have all.
Proved. NOTE: This is recorded twice in same book. E.W. (P.285)

27

Will of William NORRIS - Contested. Complainant VS James
Norris, George Norris, Samuel Norris, Stephen Norris, Thomas
Norris, Joseph Bishop, and Sarah Bishop his wife, William
Sanders and Betsy Sanders his wife, Joseph Campbell and Mulbrey
Campbell his wife, Nancy Norris, Moses Rhodes and Mary T(R?)hodes
his wife. Defendants of bill.. This cause heard of March 1818
before Hon. Alfred M. Harris, Judge and etc. when it appears
that the same was taken as confessed against William Sanders
and Betsy his wife, James Norris, Thomas Norris, Joseph Bishop
and Sarah his wife, Nancy Norris and set for hearing exparte as
to them and the answer of George Norris, Stephen Norris, Joseph
Campbell and Milbrey his wife, and Moris Rhodes and Mary his
wife etc. In answer it appears that Hannah Norris He departed
this life since bill was filed which was suggested on the record
and said court continued in name of William Norris. Now finally
heard. Testimony of Hardy Hunt and Thomas Hunt on or about
October 1814.. John Norris who at that time resided in Sumner
County departed this life a few days before his death he signed
a will as follows (Copy of will of John Norris). The will sets
out..... Wife Hannah have use of one half of plantation with
house and household goods and negroes etc. her life of widowhood.
Gives to son William Norris one half of plantation at my death
and other half at his mother's death. Rest of property divided
between rest of my children. James Norris, George Norris, Samuel
Stephen Norris, Thomas Norris, Sarah Bishop, Betsy Sanders, Mary
Rhodes, Milberry Campbell, and Nancy Norris. Appoints son William
Norris and Thomas Blackmore executors. Witnessed by Hardy Hunt
and Thomas Hunt. Fielding Greensley. Will was contested.
Sumner Co. Nov. 1818. copy of decree from Circuit Court of Sumner
Co. case Wm. Norris Compt. Vs others. (P.285-6)

Will of William MONTGOMERY Sr. - Son William, Junior, I give
negroes and furniture. Daughter Margarette Montgomery I give
negroes and etc. Son William and daughter Margarette to have
cattle, etc. Daughter Sally Watkins I give $100 paid by Mary
Martin and Nancy Wright. To daughter Nancy Martin her life land
etc. and at her death it goes to Sally Watkins. To daughter
Nancy Wright I lend negroes and etc. and at her death to Sally
Watkins. Appoints son William executor. 9 Jan. 1819. Proved
Feb. 1819 (P.288)

Will of James TROUSDALE - Sons William and Prison B.
Trousdale. Tract of land I live on 200 acres. That on the west
side of road leading to ridge called James Douglasses road to my
son William. Balance of land on East, to my wife Elizabeth her
life or widowhood and then to son Prison B. My daughter Nancy
mare and furniture and etc. My sons John Trousdale, Alexander
Trousdale, James Trousdale, Robert Trousdale, Jonathan Trousdale
and my son-in-law Caleb Williams and his wife Ann Williams.
___?___ Moore and his wife Elizabeth, Morgan Vardimin and his
wife Mary. Mathew Cowin and his wife Catherine. Mathew Neale
and his wife Sarah and my daughter Nancy Trousdale to have $10.00
each. Son William and son Prison B. executors. My sons and
sons-in-law executors also wife. 2 Sept. 1818. Proved Feb. 1819.
Wit: George Crockett, D. Fulton. (P.291)

Will of Thomas PATTON - Wife Sarah, executor to plantation as surveyed by Joseph Webb, 100 acres. Land to son John Bailey, My younger children to live with their mother until marry and land to John Bailey at his mother's death or marriage. Other property divided between my daughters. To my son William Patton plantation he lived on 80 acres. My children: Elizabeth Ormane, Jane Vinson, Mary Anderson, Sarah Gregory, Lena Cates, Lucretia Higison. My younger children Lucinda Patton and John Baily Patton. Appoints John Hamilton and Daniel Ormond and Jacob Haudyshall executors. 3 Oct. 1818. Proved Aug. 1819. (P.292)

Will of Frances KITRING - Wife Barbary Kitring her life, planta-tion. Son Peter Kiting. Part of plantation had been conveyed to son Peter and husband Toplry and James Ellis. Son Christopher Ketring. Land I bought of Leonard Dugger one acre off land I purchased of Chamberland Hudson. Son Phillip Ketring of Lancaster Co, Pa. To son Peter Ketring, Edward Ellis, Benjamine Taylor, James Elliss and Husband Tossly each $1.00. Land I purchased of Leonard Dugger. Appoints son Peter exec. with wife. 24 April 1819. Proved August 1819. (P.293)

Will of James HART - My wife to have command of home plantation. Our children. Samuel to have 160 acres adjoining River and including Ferry and all land I purchased of Thomas Donoho, on River. Children Billy and Cyrus to have all my home farm. Lot in Hartsville my mill and all land 60 acres in hill he sold. The Locks and Wright plantation to be sold. My son Windsler have $400. when of age. My Chambers place I order the widow Hart to have her life. My daughter to have no part. Part of children under age. Sons, Billy, Cyrus to live with Mother. Appoints John W. Hamilton, Wm. L. Alexander and John Mills, with my sons Sammy and Billy, executors. 8 March 1819. Proved May 1819. (P.297)

Will of Sarah CAROTHERS - Negro boy to David Wilson until negro Henry is 45 years old paying Hugh Caruthers, Thomas Caruthers, Ezekiel Caruthers and James Scott their equal parts of $300. To Ezekiel Caruthers two sons Robert and William $100. To David Wilson's son James $100. To James Scott's daughter Jane a bed. My brother Thomas daughter Sarah Jane a cow. To David Wilson's son James a cow. My sister Jane Wilson. My interest in my father's land estate to go to my Brother Ezekiel Caruthers. Appoints David Wilson Exec. 17 June 1819. Proved Aug. 1819. (P.299)

Will of Edward SANDLRS - To School children. Mentions Wife. Children under age. Daughter Polly M. Waynor. Sons Trigg and David when of age. Wife 200 acres land including place live on. Wife Lockey Sanders, Dr. John P. Wagoner and James Sanders executors. Proved in Court. Nov. 1819. (P.300)

Will of Wiley MITCHELL - Property to support father and mother Solomon and Elizabeth Mitchell. Executors to rent land. When mother and father die sell and divide estate to children of John & Elizabeth Moore and children of John & Sarah Herman. Appoints Silas Polk exec. Aug. 9, 1819. Proved Nov. 1819. (P.301)

Will of Abigail CLARK - Sick and weak. Property a good
deal of it. To be sold. Son James G. Clark. My young son
comes of age, then sell the property. Daughter Hannah,bed etc.
Son Hezekiah a counterpin. Son David calico bed quilt. Divide
between 3 youngest children, namely Hannah, David and Hezekiah.
Four children. Son James G. when of age 18 years. My children
James G, Hannah, David and Hexekiah. I wish John Cloar (? Sloan)
to take two of my children and some one else the other two.
Appoint John Sloan and James G. Sloan executors. April 7, 1818.
Proved May 1818. (P.303)

Will of Merrith J. CRENSHAW - Wife Elizabeth Crenshaw her
life or marriage. Afterwards divide equally between Isyphar and
Wm. P. Crenshaw. Feb. 1818. (P.305)

Will of Owen DILLARD - Wife Polly property, land, life.
My four sons, John, Gabriel, Willis and Alen (Olen) Dillard.
When property sold their share, Girisa White, John White, and
Jesse White to have equal parts. Three White children. My four
sons executors. 14 March 1818 probated Aug. 1818. (P.305)

Will of James DONOHO - Wife Susannah Donoho all estate
real and personal for life. When she die divide between William
Doncho, Yancey Tuner (Turner) and Nancy Meador wife of John
Meador. After death of wife divide between all children. My
daughter Betsey Gourldman Donoho called Betty Gourldman Bond
$10.00 Daughter Sally Hana Donoho $10.00. Daughter Nancy wife
of John Meador negro girl. Wife and sons executors. Dated 1820
Proved May 1820. (P.306)

Will of James C. WILSON - Wife Mary her life plantation I
live on at present, except 4 lots of each I acre (two acres taken
off of said plantation adjoining Public Road for my two daughters
Iva and Narissa ?). Two acres off of South side of said Road
for two daughters Salivia and Emalina. Estate intended for me by
my Mother in her will at decease of my Mother. To my son Franklin
Wilson at my wife's death plantation. 100 Acres plantation my
mother now lives on at her death to my daughter Iva and daughter
Manissa (Narcissa). To daughter Salivia and dau. Emaline
tract land on spring creek of Duck River in Bedford County, 400
acres. Daughter Emaline negroes. My land in Bedford County on
Falling Creek to be sold 69 acres. To son Franklin Wilson $200.
To grandson James Henderson $200. Appoints Shadrack Nye and
Jonathan Wilson executors. Aug. 5, 1818. Proved May 1820.
(P.308)

Will of William McDANIEL - Wife Martha all estate. At her
death divide among children equally. Four children. Son Joseph
McDaniel. Appoints wife and son Alfred McDaniel executors.
24 March 1820. Proved May 1820. (P.311)

Will of James CLENDENING - Son Anthony Thomas and James all
sons one third part my land. My daughter not by name, land.
Daughters Rachel, Pattsy, Eliza, and Sally to be schooled. David
Shelby and Henry Bledsoe executors. March 3, 1811. Will contested.
(P.312)

30

Will of Lewen (Lewis, Levin ?) STALLCUP - 25 March 1820. All
property to wife Barbary her life. Children to be schooled and raised
and equally divided at her death. 30 March 1820. Proved May 1820.
Deposition of Wm. Sanders, Charles Sanders and Jenny King to prove
will. Admr. granted Barbary Stallcup relict of deceased and Elijah
Stallcup enter bond with Geo. Stallcup and Jno. Wallace. (P.313)

Will of John McMURRY - Wife Elizabeth all plantation etc. To
James McMurry, negroes. To David McMurry, negroes. Daughter Peggy
McMurry negroes. To John McMurry, negroes. Samuel my son land he
lives on. Daughter Betsy McMurry negroes (she is married). Daughter
Peggy under age. Daughter Eleanor McKissack, negroes. Negroes to
Eleanor and Robert McKissack. Executors sons Samuel and John. 6 July
1820. Proved Aug. 1820. (P.314)

Will of William COWDEN - All estate to wife Lucy her life. Land I
live on. Land to daughter Susy Simpson after wife's death. Son James
has received. Son William has received. Son Josiah has received.
Appoints James Cowden and Robert Simpson executors. Nov. 11, 1811.
Proved Aug. 1820. (P.318)

Will of Richard KEY - I do give and bequeath all right and claim
and interest I am entitled to as one of heirs of Martin Keys Jr. in
Albemarle County, Virginia to my nephews John and Alexander Keys, sons
of Strother Key, also my interest in estate of John Key, deceased to
them. Appoints Zachariah Wilson Jr. exec. April 30, 1820. Proved
Aug 1820. (P.319)

Will of William P. PEARERS (PEARCE) - All estate to my Mother
Karen Pearers (Pearce) and two youngest brothers and young sister, viz,
Jonathan, Owen and Caren Pearsers (Pearce). Settle with my father
Henry Peasers. 18 June 1820. Proved Aug 1820. (P.319)

Will of Joseph WALLACE - Wife Mary one half tract land I live on
and Houses. Household etc. Should any legacy come to me from my wife's
father, I will it to my wife. Son James one half tract land due me by
Wm. Polk. Son John one half tract due of Wm. Polk. Son Samuel one half
land I live on. Daughter Mary Henold (?) negroes. My land in Christian
Co. be sold and divided between 5 daughters, Elizabeth, Sarah, Jane,
Ann and Matilda. Appoints son-in-law Wallis Harris and my son James.
Exec. July 14, 1820. Proved Nov. 1820. (P.320)

Will of Elizabeth I. ROGERS - For love and affection to my Mother
and sister. Property to four sisters. Sept. 7, 1820. Proved Nov. 1820.
(P.322)

Will of Kasper MANSKER - Wife Elizabeth Mansker part of tract of
land I live on. North of creek. Her life. To nephews George and
William Mansker sons of my brother Geo Mansker land lying on south side
of creek and 110 acres land on heard Lunsey's fork (Looney's Fork). My
niece Mary Miller daughter of my brother George Mansker and to my
nephew Lewis and John Mansker sons of my brother George rest of estate.
Appoints Isac Walton and Geo Smith exec. 31 July 1820. Proved Feb.
1821. (P.323)

31

Will of Michael CAVATT - Wife Katharine Cavatt my plantation I
live on her life or widowhood, to raise family. Four sons George,
Alexander, Thomas and Claiborne Cavatt. Two daughters Martha and
Elizabeth Cavatt. Daughter Mary Smart. Wife executor. 11 Oct.
1820. Proved July 1821. (P.324)

William BLACKARD - Wife Eliza her life. Household and etc.
She to be executor. 4 Nov. 1820. Proved Feb. 1821. (P.325)

Redmond B. BARRY - Will - Son Thomas home plantation I live
on and tract land adjoining property of Rethalls (Benthall). Son
David the mill plantation between Cumberland River. (should be
I think below Cumb. River) Wife Jane Barry her dower. Give
children education. Daughter Polly. Daughter Rachel $4000 they
under 21 years age. If wife pregrant child or children to share.
Appoints Wm. Hall and Elijah Roddie executors. Proved May 1821.
(P.326)

Will of William DOWNS - Old and weak. Wife Mary. Free
slaves. My four children son Major Downs, son William Downs,
Daughter Charity Tilly and my daughter Elizabeth Tomblin. Appoints
Wm. H. Anderson and Mebane Anderson executors. 3 March 1821.
Proved May 1821. (P.329)

Will of John BRADLEY old and infirm. Wife Mary Bradley my
land etc. Children Richard Bradley, Simpson Bradley. John
Bradley, Joshua Bradley, Jesse Bradley, and balance divided
equally between Polly Bradley and Nancy Spralling and David
Bradley. My son David live with us, he land 26 Aug. 1819.
Proved 1821. (P.330

John ROWLAND will. in a low and lingering state of body.
Children to be educated and schooled. Property divided among
family. Daughter Marind. Friend and neighbor Wm, Locke, Alexander and my brother David Rowland executors. 13 Feb. 1821.
Proved May 1821. (P.332)

Will of John WHITE - Sons Thomas and John White. My wife.
Sons James and George and Mitchell my legacy which is coming
from my father James White in Virginia. Sons Thomas and John my
land, property in Blount Co, Tenn, in possession of said John
White. Son Wilson White $1.00. Feb. 10, 1819. Signed John
White. Proved August 1821. (P.332)

Will of Richard JACKSON - Wife Jemimah Ann Jackson have land
I live on. etc. Daughter Lucretia. Son Washington Battle
Jackson. My three youngest children Polly Richardson, Francis
David Wilson Williams and Washington Battle. 25 July 1821.
Proved Aug. 1821. (P.334)

Will of James GILLIAM - Wife Frances and my children. Son
John H.Gilliam, Louisa, Milly's daughter. Son James Gilliam.
Susannah Dapuey the youngest daughter to my daughter Sarah
Hawkins Dapuey. To my daughter Polly Webb. Polly Mill's
daughter. To daughter Martha Harris, Maria Reddy's daughter.

To my son Charles H. Gilliam. To my son Taylor G.Gilliam. To my daughter Naney H. Gilliam. To my son Stephen R. Gilliam. To my daughter Susannah Woodson two sons James and Richard Woodson. To daughter Frances Patterson's children. Wife Frances. Son Charles H. Gillian, executor and my wife Frances. 11 Feby 1821. Proved Aug. 1821. (P.335)

Richard WILKS Senr. of Sumner Co. will. Daughter Jane Wynn. Daughter Anna Wynne. Wife Ann. Wife Ann. Children minors. Richard, William, Jane, Ann. Sons John and Samuel. Sons Richard and John executors. Nov. 1, 1821. Proved Nov. 1821. (P.337)

Will of Elizabeth BRACKEN widow of William, deceased. Daughter Polly Keen wife of Ashford Keen Tract land I now live on. Appoints Addison Foster executor. 5 Jan. 1819. Proved Nov. 1821. (P.338)

John RYZOR will - 5 March 1821. Son Peter 100 acres land. Daughter Mincy Davenport tract land South side Nashville Road. Where she now lives. Two daughters Sally and Polly 100 acres and adjoining Peter Ryzor. Son Thomas land. Wife Polly executris. Proved March 5, 1821. Feb. 1822. (P.339)

Will of Shelton BROWN - Wife Polly Brown. Sons Reuben I. Brown. 30 Oct. 1821. Proved Feb. 1822. (P.341)

Will of John ERWIN - wife Eliza. Daughter Polly. Son Matthew. Son Loch. Son John. Son Alfred. Son Eli. Son Franklin. Son Abner. Son Eli. Son Franklin. Son Jefferson. all equally. Sons William Loch Erwin. Wife and son Wm. Loch Irwin exec. 14 May 1821. Signed John A. (X?) Erwin. Proved May 1822. (P.342)

Will of Joseph TOWNSEND - Wife Mary land I live on. All children not 21 years of age. School children. Son John. Son Henry. Son Joseph. Son Peter. Son Washington. Daughter Sarah. Daughter Jane. Daughter Lucy. Daughter Mary Ann. Son John. 12 Sept. 1821 proved. (P.343)

Will of David Hardy RICKMAN - 16 May 1822 wife Peggy. Daughter Malinda Elvira Rickman. Daughter Polly Ann Rickman. Brother Thomas Rickman. Brother-in-law William Henry, executor. Brother-in-law Moses H. Henry guardian to daughter. Proved May 1822. (P.345)

James VINSON will - Wife Rhoda plantation I live on and house. Son Stockley. Son Beuthall (Benthall). Son James. My children. Daughter Parthena McCall. Son Enos. Money coming from Joseph White to me for a negro sold at Orleans. Daughter Susannah Hamilton. To my illegimate son Edmond called Edmond Vinson all land where on the said Edmond now lives 80 (84) acres. called Walnut Field. Owns lots in Town of Cairo. Granddaughter Eveline daughter of Benthall Vinson. Daughter Parthenia McCall and Susannah Hamilton land in Warren County. Appoints Thomas Anderson and my three sons Enos, James and Stockley executors. 24 July 1818. Proved. Codicil. July 24, 1818 land I purchased of William S. Patton mentioned. Gives illigamate son Edmond 400 acres land being on Perry Fork of Tidewater in Lexington Kentucky. Speaks of land purchased from Isaac Gregory 50 acres. Proved May 1822 (P.347)

David SHELBY will - Two youngest sons Orville Shelby and Albert Shelby tract land whereon I now live 1363 acres. Land in Davidson County opposite town of Nashville. Two oldest sons John Shelby and Anthony R. Shelby by deed. All children not of age. Youngest son Albert will be 18 years of age on 25 May 1826. Sons John, Anthony R. land at Huntsville, Franklin Co, Alabama. Three daughters land in Territory of Illinois. Town property in Gallatin. Daughter Lucinda Henderson. Daughter Eleanor Desha. Daughter Sally R. Fearn. Mentions books. Wife Sally. Tract land part of Greenfield tract which was devised to my wife by will of her father. Mentions a bible to wife. Children: John, Anthony R., Lucinda Henderson, Elenor Desha. Orville Shelby. Sally Fearn. Albert Shelby. Granddaughter Priscilla Douglass daughter of my deceased daughter Priscilla. Mentions Wm. Little of White Co. partner. Mentions Wm. Little of White Co. partner of my said son. Mentions Salt Works in White Co. Mentions Bank stock. Mentions Thomas Perry of Caroline Co, Va. Codicil Sept. 1822. (P.352)

Will of Samuel SELLERS of Williamson County, State of Mississippi. Wife and children. Aug. 23, 1822. Proved Nov. 1822. Appoints wife and Edward McGuire, executors. (P.361)

Will of David MAHAN Sr. - 8 Oct. 1822. Land I live on bequeth to my sons David and James. Mentions note against James Lackey $302.39 Daughters Sarah Mahan. Grandson David Cline. Mentions Sarah, David, and James Mahan. John and Alexander Mahan. James Lacey. Daughter Eleander. Appoints James Durham, Fielding Bryson, executors. Proved Nov. 1822. (P.361)

Samuel HART will - Three brothers William H. Hart, Cyrus Hart, Winston Hart. All money coming to me from my father's estate. All money coming to me from the sale of our lands. agreeable to my father's will. My three brothers and my mother. My sister Cynthia Hart. My sister Polly P. Lauderdale my plantation. Appoints brother-in-law William Lauderdale and Wm. L. Alexander executors. 29 Aug. 1822. Proved Nov. 1822. (P.363)

Will of John H. BOWEN of town of Gallatin. Mentions "family" but not by each name. Appoints brother Samuel A. Brown (?) and Wm. L. Alexander executors 18 Sept. 1822. Proved Nov. 1822. (P.364)

Daniel BENTHALL will of sound mind. Wife Frances. Children not by name but mentioned as children. 15 Aug. 1822. Proved Aug. 1822. Mentions land belonging to my wife which was the legacy by my wife lying on waters of Station Camp to be sold. (P.365)

Sarah HART will - Estate of James Hart referred to. I have 1/5 part. Son Samuel Hart. My four sons divide interest in estate of James Hart. Sons William, Samuel, Cyrus 1/4. Winslow Hart. Mentions the family Bible. Daughter Polly Lauderdale. Daughter Cynthia. My brother John W. Hamilton executor. Proved May 1823. (P.366)

Agness MARTIN will - nephew Jimerson Bandy crops. 15 Nov. 1820. Proved May 1823. (P.369)

34

Alfred M. DOUGLASS will - Wife Cherry and three children names James, Lucy and William. Wife executor. 28 Jan. 1822. Proved Aug. 1822. (P.370)

Will of William HALE - Daughter Elizabeth Young deed. to her children. Daughter Sarah Williams, and her children. Appoints Priscila Hale, Cage Hale and William Hale executors. 24 June 1821. Proved Aug. 1822. (P.371)

Will of Henry PHILLIPS - Wife Elizabeth. No children by name but referred to. 3 April 1820. Proved 1822. (P.372)

Jeremiah BELOTE will - Sept. 14. 1816. My brother John Belote. To John I. Swaney $10.00. My sister Ann Swaney $20.00. To James Stewart $60.00. To Peggy Stewart $40.00. My four children Sally, Jeremah, John and Clarissa Ann. To Mrs. Louise Stewart will my plantation tools. Children not all of age. I appoint my father Harry D Belote, Wm. Cage and Wm. Smith my executors. Proved Aug. 1822. (P.373)

William REDDITT - January 9, 1823, Pvd. May 1823 Will - Wife
Fanny Redditt.   (P.96)

Elizabeth HOUSE - December 31, 1816 Will - Granddaughter
Polly Williamson Axum, who is the Daughter of my daughter Sarah
SHOTE. Grandson Elias Briant Axum. Five children: Marajah
House, John House, Jacob House, Sarah Shote, Patty Axum. Executor
James Gwin. Proved May 1823. (P.1)

William BENNETT - 24 March 1823 Will - Wife. 200 acres land.
Divided between Elisha 80 acres at mother's death, Richard and
William. My 10 children. Not all called by name. Sons Elisha,
Richard and William Bennett. Executors. Proved May 1823. (P.2)

Abraham EKOLS - March 30, 1823 Will - Wife Nancy. Proved May
1823. (P.3)

Matthew ALEXANDER - 5 September 1823 Will - Wife Elizabeth.
Son James. Son Stephen. Son Edwin. Son David. Daughter Prudence
Snoddy. My son David and wife Elizabeth executors. Proved Nov.
1823. (P.3)

John DICKERSON - March 4, 1823 Will - Wife Mary. Son William.
Made a division of estate 1816 to part of the children. Daughter
Sarah Haues. (Haws). Daughter Nancy P. Stovall. Son John H. Dickerson.
Mentions Blacksmith tools. Daughter Elizabeth Tendall. Daughter
Rebecca L. Shelton. Son Ellis A. Dickerson. Son Hartwell S. Dickerson.
Proved 1823 Nov. (P.3)

Charlotte COLE - July 7, 1822 Will - To Daniel Allen property in
Sumner Co. Proved Aug. 1823. (P.6)

Charlotte BARRETT - July 26, 1823 Will - Daughter-in-law Mary
Barratt. Daughter Sally Barratt. Daughter Elizabeth Barratt. Son
Jacob Barrett. Son John Barrett. Appointed John McElwrath exec.
Proved Aug. 1823. (P.7)

Jesse FLIPPIN - February 10, 1821 Will - Wife Mildred Flippin.
Children Poley, Isaac, Mildred and Betsy. Friend Elijah Robertson and
wife Mildred. Proved Feby. 1824. (P.7)

Asa HODGE - October 23, 1823 Will - Wife Jemima. Sons Ransom S.
Son Creed C. ' Son Asa M. Son Alfred J. Proved Nov. 1823. (P.8)

John KENNEDY - August 14, 1823 Will - Daughter Emily. Three children not called by name. Sons Prior and son Preston. Mentions his
father's estate. Appoints James Williamson and Daniel Kennedy executors.
Proved Nov. 1823. (P.9)

37

Samuel BRILEY - November 5, 1822 Will - Wife. Sons James and John. Son William. Daughter Nancy Summers wife of Cornelius Summers. Daughter Betsy MINOR. Daughter Polly SUMMERS. Appoints Edward Morgan executor. Proved Feb. 1824. (P.10)

William WHITE - March 24, 1820 Will - Son Robert White. Daughter Elizabeth TELSINGER. Son Charles H. White. Son Robert White. Daughter Fanny White. Daughter Sally Dickeson. Proved May 1824. (P.12)

Adam HUNTER - May 6, 1823 Will - Eldest son Edward. Wife Gilly P. Second son Layton. Third son Lemuel S. Eldest daughter Charlotte Hunter. Second daughter Luncenda. Children: Silas M. Hunter. David Hunter. Gilly P. Hunter. Land in Madison Co, Tenn. Proved Aug. 1824. (P.13)

Thomas JOYNER - March 10, 1824 Will - Son Littleton. Son Thomas. Son Absolam. Wife Milley. Daughter Sally White. Daughter Elizabeth Traber. Daughter Winifred Abston. Wife Milley. Proved Aug. 1824. (P.15)

Elizabeth DICKINS - June 14, 1824 Will - Grandson Josiah PERRY. Grandson Isaac PERRY. Granddaughter Ann PAKER. Son-in-law John PERRY. Daughter Charity PERRY. Son Isaac BAKER. Grandson King Luton. Grandson Leonard PERRY. Appoints Isaac Walton executor. Proved Nov. 1824. (P.16)

William HAMMOND - February 4, 1816 Will - Wife Jane. Wife Jane and John McMurtry executors. Proved Nov. 1824. (P.17)

Thomas STARKS - August 26, 1824 Will - Wife Celia. My children not called by name. Proved Nov. 1824. (P.18)

William WHITE - August 8, 1824 Will - Son Alexander A. Sons, William and Lewis land in Humphreys Co. Daughter Elizabeth, Elizabeth Moore a woman now living with me. Proved Nov. 1824. (P.19)

William HUBERT - April 24, 1824 Will - Wife Sarah. Daughter Polly Cloar. Grandchildren: Elizabeth Cloar. Hubert Cloar. Calvin Cloar. William Cloar. Daughter Elizabeth Little. Son Benjamine Hubert. Son John Hubert. Son David Hubert. Proved Nov. 1824. (P.20)

Caty DOTSON - November 7, 1824 Will - Son Edward S. Daughter Betsy Gifte. Daughter Stephenson M. Green. Children, Nancy, Ellis, June TURNER (?) and Betsy Gifte. Also William Dotson and Polly BOTTRIP. Also Araline ARNOLD and Edward S. Dotson. Proved Feb. 1825. (P.22)

Nelson FURGERSON - May___ 1825 Will - Wife. (P.23)

Thomas SEAWELL - January 10, 1825 Will - Thomas Seawell will. Wife Mary Seawell. Daughter Abigail M. Son Benjamine C. Son John B. Son Jeremiah P. Son Robert H. Daughter Martha T. Daughter Eliza F.B. Wife Mary. Proved May 1825. (P.24)

George Washington W.W. TOWNSEND - Will - Stepmother Lucrecy
Townsend. Half brother Joseph W.W. Townsend. Half sister Elizabeth N.
Townsend. Half brother Peter Townsend, Jr. Appoints Thomas Stone and
John Wilks, executors. May 21, 1825. Proved Aug. 1825 (P.25)

Thomas STUBBLEFIELD - July 18, 1819 Will - Thomas Stubblefield.
Will. Wife Nancy. Land on road from Bledsoe's Lick to Hartsville.
Children: Anstreat Stubblefield, George; Woodruff; Fanny BRADLEY,
Tilman; Elizabeth BRADSHAW, Nancy WALTON, Lucindy, Garrison. Fanny
married Col. Edward Bradley. Armstreet died and left infant daughter
Amelia H. Stubblefield. Proved 1825. (P.26)

Hector WILLIAMS - March 31, 1825 Will - Oldest son Benjamine J.
Wife Jane and Benj. F. Williams, executors. Proved Aug. 1825. (P.31)

Catherine PAYNE - January 30, 1821 Will - Daughter Betsy Jefferson.
Daughter Catherine Jefferson. Son Mathew Baine. Daughter Nancy Payne.
Daughter Nancy Payne only executor. Proved Aug. 1825. (P.31)

Joseph McLEURATH Sr. - February 23, 1816 Will - Wife Elizabeth.
Son William. Son John. Son Joseph. Five Daughters: Nancy ROGERS,
Gean ORR, Sally ORR, Mary WILSON, Rebeckah ALEXANDER. Wife executor
with son William. Proved Aug. 1825. (P.32)

Richard BROWN - October 12, 1824 Will - Only daughter named as
Rebecca PUCKETT. Son Armstead Brown. Wife Elizabeth executor.
Grandchildren: Lydia Eliza Brown, Samuel C. Brown who are the son and
daughter of my son John Brown. Proved 1825 Aug. (P.33)

John PARKER - June 13, 1825 Will - Wife Rody. Son Noah Parker.
Son William. Son John. Daughter Rody Short. Son Wiley. Daughter
Susan Parker. Daughter Scully Parker. Daughter Eliza Parker.
Daughter Matilda Parker. Grandson Vardeman Parker. Wife Rody execu-
tor. Proved Aug. 1825. (P.34)

Benjamine RAWLINGS - August 14, 1825 Will - Edward G. Rawlings.
Elenor HOWARD. Margaret Rawlings. Alexander H. Rawlings. Letitia
Rawlings. Bennett A. Rawlings. Rufus King Rawlings. Geo. Washington
Rawlings. Does not call them his children but it is indicated.
Deceased wife to have a fence built around her grave, and a rock at
her grave. Son-in-law James HOWARD and Col. Lewis Green guardian for
son Rufus King Rawlings and daughter Benneta Rawlings and son Geo
Washington Rawlings. Executors Co. Lewis and son-in-law James HOWARD.
Proved Nov. 1825. (P.35)

Will of Benjamine RAWLINGS - August 6, 1825 - To Edward G.
Rawlings, Elmer Howard, Margaret Rawlings, Alexander H. Rawlings,
Lillian Rawlings, Bennetta Rawlings, Rufus King Rawlings and George
Washington Rawlings. My land conveyed to me by Archibald Marlin
11 May 1822. Constitute my son-in-law James Howard and Col. Lewis
Green guardian to my son Rufus King Rawlings, my daughter Bennetta
Rawlings and my son George Washington Rawlings. 14 Aug. 1825. Witnesses
Zachariah Green and Elisha Long. (P.35

Will of George F. KEESEE - Wife land her widowhood. Land whereon
my son George F. Keesee lives. My daughter Larrie (Laree) Smith.
Daughter Patience Smith. Daughter Roda McKnight. Son Thomas Keessee.
Daughter Agnes Lyon. Her son Champress Bell (Ball). Daughter Nancy
Henry. Son George F. Keessee. To Robert Saunders for my daughter
Jane Saunders deceased heirs former wife (his former wife). My
grandson George Saunders 135 acres. Residue divided between my
children Lane Smith, Patience Smith, Rody McKnight, Agnes Lyon,
Abednia Bull (Ball), Nancy Henry, George F. Keesee. Executors
George F. Keessee and Wm. Henry. Proved Nov. 1825. (P.36)

Will of Richard C. TYREE - Wife Mary, negroes and land I live
on to be sold and wife and children to have a suitable residence.
Also to be educated. When daughters or son arrives at age etc.
Son William. 200 acres port of Robertson and Spring Tract. Appoits
wife Mary and my brother Pleasant Tyree executors. 20 Aug. 1825.
Proved Nov. 1825. (P.37)

Will of Moses JONES - Appoints John Cryer executor. Wife
Priscilla. Sept. 22, 1824. Proved May 1826. (P.38)

Will of Jessee JOHNSON - Daughter Elizabeth Roberts $5.00.
Daughter Sally Johnson. Daughter Mary Teely. $5.00 Son Matthew.
Daughter Charlotte Blackmore. Dau. Rebecca Blackmore. Grandson
Jesse Johnson Finley my French watch. Land I live on adjoining
town of Cairo held by deed from Richard Cook and David Wilson Senr.
late of this county. Son Mathew Johnson and my son-in-law Obadiah
Gaines Tinly (Finley) exec. 10 April 1824. Proved May 1826. (P.39)

Will of William BRASEL - Sick. My beloved wife Margaret land
we live on with other etc. Divide between heirs Julia Edward my
oldest daughter. Daughter Polly Brasel. Daughter Margaret Brasel.
Son William land on Duck River to Sons Benjamine and Wiley. My
will is Henry T. Brasel have a horse. My son Wiley not 21 years
age. Appoints Thomas Miers exec. and my wife Margaret. 2 Feb.
1826. Proved May 1826. (P.40)

Will of Jarratt DURNAL (DARNAL) - Son John S. Darnal negroes
etc. land. Son William. Other property divided between John Sand,
William Darnal, etc. My grandson Francis Darnal $100.00. To
Sally Hardy a decent maintenance by my sons Jno. and William Darnal.
Son John S. Darnal exec. Sept. 30, 1822. Proved May 1826. (P.41)

Will of Anthony SWEAT - Wife Hannah one half land etc. To
my stepson John Grooms one half of land etc. Appoints friend John
Shaver, exec. May 1, 1825. Proved May 1826. (P.42)

Will of Robert DAVIS, Senr. - Wife Sarah all perishable
property. My two daughters Nancy Lowery and Esther Lowery. Mentions a family bible. Other property to son, Robert and mentions
especially Fisher's & Erskine Catichism. To son William some
perishable property. Son Archibald Davis $1.00. My daughter Mary
Reed $1.00. My children Robert Davis, Wm. David, John Davis,
Margaret Reed, Sarah Durham, and Elizabeth Denny. Appoints James
Kirkpatrick executor. Sept. 1, 1825. Proved Feb. 1826. (P.43)

40

Will of James WINCHESTER - Have Masonic burial. Wife Susan
Winchester 5 old negroes and part of land I live on, to educate and
support our children now living with us. Should wife be pregrant to
raise it in like manner. Rest property disposed of. Appoints wife and
Lucillius Winchester and Wm. Cage executors. No. date. Proved Aug.
1826. (P.43)

Will of Ira TATUM - Wife Patsy. Household and etc. land to be
sold. My children William Parnet, Alfred Carroll, Abner Marion Tatum.
to be educated to read write and arithmetic. My daughter Eliza Ann
Tatum to read and write. Three sons not yet 15 years of age. Appoints
Dabney Tatum and John Eddins exec. July 24, 1826. Proved Aug. 1826.
(P.44)

Will of James BROWN - Wife Margaret household goods, etc. Son
Samuel to have at wife's death. Daughter Elenor Brown $150. I leave
my wife if she lives longer than he mother also my will and desire is
if Alithon Brown lives with my son Samuel Brown till 21 years old to be
schooled. Dau Mary Cre, $1.00 and other property. Son John Brown
$1.00 and property. Daughter Jane Horton $1.00 and etc. Daughter
Nacissa Horton $1.00 etc. Daughter Eunice Horton $1.00 etc. Son
Samuel Brown $1.00 etc. Wife and son Samuel Brown executors. 15 May
1826. Proved Aug. 1826. (P.45)

Will of Joseph M. BULLUS merchant of town of Gallatin. My mother
Elizabeth Bullins (Bullus) had a note against me for $5000 I wish to be
settled. My wife and children now born or she may bear me. Store in
Gallatin continue if possible by my friend Mr. Edward Stratton. Wife
Sarah G. Bullus to sell enough to pay debts and she to receive rest of
profits. Appoints friend Alfred H. Douglass and Robert M. Boyers
executors. 18 Sept. 1825. Proved 1826 Nov. (P.46)

Will of William PITTMAN - Land purchased from executors of James
Stewart to be sold for debts and best interest of my children. Daughter
Betsy Moore to have negroes. Son John B. Pittman negroes. Son Hutchins
Minus Pittman to have negroes. My minor children under age. Son Wm. F.
Four children Mary Jane, James Fountain, Martha B. and Sarah Susannah
Pittman. (P.47)

Will of William PITTMAN - To land purchased from executors of
James Stewart to be sold and used as best for young children. Daughter
Betsy Moore. Son John C. Pittman. Son Hutchens Minus Pittman. Some
of children minors. Son William F. Pittman. Four youngest children
Mary Jane Pittman, James Fountain Pittman, Martha B. Pittman, and Sarah
Susannah Pittman. My sister Nancy Jones wife of Lucellin Jones of
Alabama has been desirous to take my daughter B. Pittman and adopt her
as her own now in care of Mrs. Jones so if she takes Martha B. and gives
property equal to value of others. (Mrs. Jones was Martha's Aunt.
(M.B.'s) (Mr. Jones M.B.'s uncle). Sept. 26, 1826. Executor Wm.
Glover and my son John B. Pittman. Proved. (P.47)

Will of John BELOTE - Wife Patsy plantation I live on and to
school children if she marry to have one third. Children not by name.
William Cage and John L. Swaney executors. 26 Aug. 1826. Proved. (P.48)

Will of Anthony B. REID - Wife Henrietta property life.   Exec.
Robert W. Sanford. 5 Oct. 1826. Proved Nov. 1826. (P.49)

Will of Coleman PARKER - Wife Mollie land in my possession left
to me by my father deceased. My mother's death and all personal
property. Her life and at death to my son Thomas J. Parker. Wife
Mollie exec. 9 Aug. 1826. Proved Nov. 1826. (P. 50)

Will of Isham HODGES Junior - Appoints Meredith Hodges Executor.
Wife Sarah and my seven children (Daniel. Stokes Hodges, Samuel
Woodrid Hodges, Mullissey L. Hodges, Marquis A. Hodges, and Harriet
L. Hodges, Sanford P. Hodges, and Clarissa M. Hodges. Sept. 1,
1826. Proved Nov. 1826. (P.50/51)

Will of William HEART - Wife Lucy G. Heart all. The land
which I devise from her father's estate my wife is authority to
dispose of my part. She to possess and dispose at her death as
she wishes, My sister Cyntyia Allison at death of my wife one
third. My brother Winslow Heart 2/3 at death of my wife. My
brother Cyrus Heart tract land I live on including mills and
cotton gin town property and etc. My sister Polly Lauderdale
$5.00. Brother Samuel Heart. I provide for maintenance and English
education to be given to William Y. Goodale. 2 Oct. 1826. Proved
Nov. 1826. (P.51)

William HAYNIE's will - Wife Margaret N. Daughter Mary
Haynie under age. Daughter Mary Elizabeth should she desire,
under age. Her mother Margaret N. Appoints my father Jesse
Haynie executor. 27 June 1826. Proved Nov. 1826. (P.52)

Will of William DOSS - Wife Nancy plantation whereon I live
and etc. Some children not of age. Plantation to be in care of
Jacob Bohein and John L. Doss if wife marry and they to be executors. Children some are girls. not by name. No date. Proved
1826. (P.53)

Will of Stephen CANTRELL - Wife Mary her widowhood, plantation
etc. Executor Stephen Cantrill Jr., William Cantrill, William
Edwards son of Nathan Edwards and Zionlow Cantrill. To son Stephen
Cantrill Jr. heirs, land in Wilson Co. on Cumberland River 120
acres patented No. 4307 and 4308. also 1/3 lot No. 73 in Nashville,
Davidson Co. etc. Daughter Sarah Willis wife of Calbb Willis, 150
acres patent in name of William Bowen on North side Cumberland
River in Sumner Co. adjoining Jesse Garrett, etc, and deeds and
transfer made to me by heirs of David Carson and adjoining tract
heretofore conveyed to said Sarah Willis on West of Mose River,
etc. To children of my son Ota Cantrell tract land 264 acres
east fork Stone River commonly known as Andrews Branch in Rutherford Co. My son William Cantrell and that part of Wilkerson's
tract land that lies west and south of Station Camp Creek in
Sumner Co. and lot in town of Gallatin, Sumner Co. known by Lot
No. 9. To son Zebulon Cantrill an equal division with his brother
Darly H. Cantrill of 1574 acres in five different tracts North
side Cumberland River opposite mouth of Oly (Obey) River in
Jackson Co. and 1/3 part of lot No. 73 in Nashville, Davidson Co.

To my daughter Mary Edwards wife of William Edwards son of Nathan Edwards, her heirs to have one half of Lot No. 9 in Gallatin, Sumner Co. and land on fork of Station Camp. Other lands on Obey River in Jackson Co. and lot 73 in Nashville. To son James Madison Monroe Cantrill 411 acres land Rutherford Co. on Stewart Creek and 640 acres tract granted by North Carolina being where my son Oto now lives. My son George Clinton Cantrill one half of home plantation in Madison Creek, Sumner Co. Sons James and George not of age. Dec. 5, 1823 proved, addition to will dated 26 Aug. 1824. Annexed is "Should wife Mary marry she to have one horse and cattle, bed and furniture and surrender rest, Tract land 150 acres granted to tract tofore bequeathed to daughter Sarah Willis including house whereon Mathew Nice lived". And Sarah to have place on which Wm. Edwards formerly lived on Station Camp. 7 Jan. 1826. Codicil 6 April 1826. A law suit against Moly Mary N. Bowen and Samuel A. Brown Circuit Court Sumner Co. commenced by me against David S. Willis. Codicil. I loaned $1000 to Wm. Edwards further mention of land on Station Camp Creek. Nov. 11, 1826. Proved Feb. 1827. (P.54)

Will of William GWINN - Son Ezekiel Gwinn land South of Dry Fork 60 acres. Daughter Elizabeth Wilkerson land she now lives on 60 acres. Son James Gwinn land he lives on 100 acres. Granddaughter Elizabeth Gwinn negroes and land on North side Dry Fork adjoining John McNiells farm, containing 60 acres. Wife Hannah, land I live on. Son William Gwinn land on ridge in road that leads from Cairo to BRACKENS by Johnson Gap containing 150 acres. Three sons James, William and Ezekiel Gwinn and son-in-law Penjamine Wilkerson my saw mill equally. My granddaughter Elizabeth. I also give my wife Genevieve one years provisions. Appoints son James Gwinn and George McGuire executors. 9 Jan. 1827. Proved Feb. 1827. (P.60)

Will of John HASSELL - Son Asa. Son Jesse. Daughter Ann Worthington. Son-in-law William King. Daughter Orphan Harden. Son Asa's mother Ann Hassell. Children Asa and Jesse Hassell, Ann Worthington, Wm. King and Orphan Hardin. Appoint Asa Hassell and Wm. King executors 24 May 1825. Proved Feb. 1827. (P.61)

Will of James SANDERS - Wife Lucerissa everything in her hands and raise children. Appoints one or two of my sons guardian for rest. Son William James Sanders under age. My six children Livisa and Mary Handley, Tabitha Moore, William Brown, James Yancey, John Henry and Samuel Adams Sanders. My children by my first wife. I leave out of will. Proved Jan. 17, 1826. (P.62)

Will of Charles LATIMORE - Proved by oath of Lewis Haynie. Charles Latimore of Sumner Co. weak in body etc. make will. Wife Mary Latimore one fifth part of all. My oldest son Nicholas Latemore 60 acres 14 acres of which is out of my 60 acre tract, part he Nicholas lives on now. Rest to two sons Edwin and Oliver Latimore on condition they pay to my son George S. Lattimore $300. My daughter Harriett Latimore. My wife Mary. My three married daughters Caroline Looney, Sarah McKitchen and Lucretia Joyner each to have $2.00. Executors Edwin Latimore. Feb. 19, 1827. Proved May 1827. (P.63)

Will of Henry BELOTE - Wife Harriett one third of land I live on. My two grandsons James M. Swaney and Henry G. Belote. My four grand-

children to wit. Jeremiah Belote, John Belote, Sally Smith, and
Clarissa Belote, children of deceased son Jeremiah Belote. To
Sally Smith $5.00 and to each of the other last above named their
grandchildren Jeremiah Belote, John Belote, and Clarissa Belote
$50.00. To my grandchild Elizabeth B. Swaney $5.00. To children
of John Belote deceased and children of John L. Swaney. Children
of John Belote decd and one half of John L. Swaney, namely, James
W. Swaney, Caroline W. Swanyney, Moriah E. Swaney, Harry B. Swaney,
Mary M. Swaney and Patsy P. Swaney. It is further my will that
should Nancy Belote daughter of John Belote decd. marry George W.
Blackmore that she said Nancy is only to receive from my executors
$5.00. My daughter Ann Swaney wife of John L. Swaney $5.00. Two
grandsons James M. Swaney and Henry A. Belote a tract of land I
live on now after death of wife Harriett including Ferry known by
name Belote's Ferry and 18 acres land in South side Cumberland
River and my distillery. To grandson Henry S. Swaney land in
Sumner Co. Mentions families of John S. Swaney, Patsy Belote,
John Ward and my wife Harriett shall cross the said Ferry without
charge of Ferriage. I wish to be interred in Masonic order at
will and the Fraternity and etc. Appoints John L. Swaney, William
Cage and Licillias Winchester executors. 18 Feb. 1827. Codicil
12 March 1827. Proved May 1827. (P.64)

Will of William WHERRY Sr. - Daughter Elizabeth Fonville.
Daughter Anna Bass. Son Simon Wherry $4.00. Grandson Simon Bass
$200. Grandson John J. Wherry son of William T. Wherry, planta-
tion I live on 176 acres. Appoints William T. Wherry guardian
for his son John J. Wherry. To Simon Wherry and Sion Bass
property. Appoints Wm. T. Wherry and Zachariah Wilson executors.
Nov. 13, 1823 proved. Codicil. Will of William Wherry Sr. 13 Nov
1823 appoints my son William T. Wherry guardian for his son John
J. Wherry and the said William T. Wherry and Zachariah Wilson,
Exec. Proved May 1827. (P.66/67)

Will of Mary H. BOWEN - Sons William R. Bowen and Samuel A.
Bowen. 100 acres adjoining Diemer formerly Dedricks corner and
adjoining Cantrell's line. Daughter Louisa Sanders. Deceased
son John H. Bowen (mismanagement of his father's estate). Son
William R. Bowen and son Samuel A. Bowen 100 acres. Daughter
Celia W. Stone. Sons William Rand Bowen and Samuel A. Bowen.
My three grandchildren Mary H. Bowen, William Grant Bowen, and
John H. Bowen infant heirs of my son John H. Bowen, land in
Sumner Co. Rest divided my five children and grandchildren
Louisa Sanders, Catherine Campbell, William R. Bowen, Samuel A.
Bowen, Celia M. Stone, and my grandchildren Mary H. Bowen, Wm.
Grant Bowen, and John H. Bowen. My land estate in Kentucky
either sold or for benefit of grandchildren. Appoints sons
William R. Bowen and Samuel A. Bowen executors. Witnesses
Hoabland Sanders, Chloe Sanders, H. Russell. Daughter Catherine
Campbell. Daughter Tabotha Moore negroes and family Bible.
3 April 1827. My brother Hendley Russell one bed and clothes.
April 16, 1825. Proved May term 1827. (P.68)

Will of Alamon TRIGG - My minor children remain in possession
of my wife Lucy and certain property already bequeath to son John

Trigg, money and property. To son William have bequeathed what he is to have. Son Alanson to put in stock for him with his brother William $3000. To Alanson $1128 in money. To daughter Sally negroes, one fourth tract land divided with her three sisters when she of age or marrys. Daughter Nancy. Daughter Lucy Jane. Daughter Polly. These last three daughters 997 acres and 200 acres land on river Sumner Co. Cage Bend 640 acres in Wilson Co. on Fall Creek, and 157 acres on Stones River in Warren Co. Son James 300 acres on Stones Creek in Wilson Co. and 320 acres in Madison Co. on Johnson Creek I bought of my son Wm. Trigg and negroes. Son Henry and son Stephen 540 acres land on Bartons Creek and 640 acres in Spring Creek both in Wilson Co. to be divided. Son Alexander at death of wife Lucy plantation I live on containing all the land formerly belonging to my father's plantation and which I purchased of Col. Geo. Smith. My wife Lucy east of property. Appoints James Sanders and my wife Lucy Trigg and my sons Wm. and Alanson executors, 5 Sept. 1826. Daughter Nancy Chenault. Son-in-law Felix R. Chenault. Dec. 8, 1826. Proved May 1827. (P.70)

Will of Prudence STARK - Memorandum of. She died on 26 of present month. Property divided brother and sister. About six years ago she applied to her brother Alexander Stark to build her a house near his for her and a younger sister to live in and to take care of while she lived. Sister Charlotte Starke to have at my death. Proved Aug. 1827. (P.73)

Will of James DEFREES - Wife Sophe Defrees. land I live on, etc. Son Ashou Defrees $40. etc. Daughter Elizabeth wife of Charles Frady $1.75. Son James. Daughter Rebecca. Son John $1.75. Daughter Hannah the wife of David Hart. Son David. Son Moses. Daughter Nancy wife of Edward Williams $1.75. Daughter Polly wife of James Stovall. Son Ridley land where Edward Williams now lives. Son Joseph some land. Rest divided between sons Aricely and Joseph. Appoints wife and Wm. Austin executors. 26 July 1820. Proved Aug. 1827. Signed James Defrees. (P.73)

Will of William PATTON - Wife Ann all land including that purchased of Robert Patton, but not in possession until said Robt. 150 acres. Two sons Hiram and Napolian when of age. They be educated. All my children not be name. Appoints Joseph Kirkpatrick of Wilson County and Elijah Poddie of Sumner Co. executors. Sept. 1, 1826. Proved Aug. 1827. (P.75)

Will of Peter FISHER - Negroes to be free. My land divided. My brothers and sisters children. To Peter Buson and John Patterson Jr. exec. 31 July 1827. Proved Aug. 1827. (P.75)

Will of Lott WOOD - 20 January 1826 - Wife Mary. Youngest sons Gideon Wood and Ely Wood. Willie Wood land. Mentions Jacob Gregory, William Hurfree and Ezekial Inman. Names sons Gideon, Eli and Willie exec. Proved Aug. 1827. (P.76)

Will of William EDWARDS - Daughter Loveny Mitchell negroes. To grandson Prisley Hassell negroes. To granddaughter Charlotte Grear negroes. To Harriet Looney. My four grandchildren, children of deceased son William Edwards. To Montalbat, Richard and William land in Bledsoe County. My grandson Monatalbot Edwards negroes. My grandson Richard

45

Edwards negroes. My grandson William Edwards negroes. My granddaughter Malvina Edwards negroes. To my youngest daughter Sally
Douglass a tract land. Son-in-law Rubin Douglass and son-in-law
Wm. H. Douglass exec. Sally married Wm. H. Douglass. Oct. 20,
1827. Proved Feb. 1827. (P.77)

Will of Jesse DANIEL - Wife Ann Daniel. Daughter Mary J.
Daniel all property. Appoints John Cotton and Noah Cotton as
executors. 5 April 1826. Proved Nov. 1827. (P.79)

Will of Cabel WILLIS late of County of Overton, Tennessee.
Wife Sarah Willis. Property in Sumner Co. Son Richard Wanly
Willis $150. Sons Cabel Daniel, Malicki and my daughters Nancy,
Sarah and Lina and heirs of my son Moses deceased. Oct. 1, 1827.
Proved Nov. 1827. (P.80)

Will of Lewis CRANE - Heirs of William Crane deceased 50
acres land whereon Henry Wright now lives but said Wright and
wife Susannah have use of same her natural life. Son Caleb
Crane plantation he lives on. Two nieces Betsy Pillony and Nancy
Pillony. Appoints Ezekial Crane, Wm. Crane and Caleb Crane
executors. 4 Sept. 1827. Proved Nov. 1827. (P.81)

Will of Richard BRADLEY - Wife Catherine land I live on, etc.
on west side Drake Creek. To wife and then to daughter Catherine
Standley, land east ridge Drakes Creek. To son Isaac Bradley
land. Sons: David Pradley, William Pradley, Abram Bradley.
Isaac Bradley and the heirs of my son Richard Pradley Jr. Wish
Richard Cage, Wm. Lambeth and Abram Bradley executors. 6 Oct
1821. Proved Nov. 1827. (P.81)

William PATTON will - Sell portion of estate. To wife Ann
all estate, land I live on including 30 acres purchased of Robert
Patton but not in possession until his the said Robert's death
150 acres. Had many negroes. At wife's death to be divided
between two sons Hiram and Napolian (not of age). Rest estate
divided among my children as arrive at age. Appoints Joseph
Kirkpatrick of Wilson Co. and Elijah Foddie of Sumner Co. as
executors. 1 Sept. 1826. Proved. (P.81)

Will of William STUBBLEFIELD - My sister Francis and my
niece Sarah S. Sullivan equal share my plantation etc. furniture,
etc. Sally Martin mentioned. Mentions James H. Glasgow and
Wm. Alexander as exec. Appoints my Brother John Stubblefield
and Harris Walton as executors and guardian. Sept. 4, 1827.
Proved Nov. 1857. (P.82)

Will of Isaac GRIMM - 3 Dec. 1826 - Property held together
by wife for 3 children until son Alexander shall have age 21.
Wife Sarah Grimm one third part of all land including my dwelling.
N.H.Goods. My daughter Margaret E. Grimm my clock and when Margaret
arrives at age of 18 years I will and bequeath to her the named
negroes etc. To Alexander G. Grimm and Charles J. Grimm each a
writing desk. Alexander B. (under age 21). Children to have
English education. Appoints Daniel Montgomery and Willie J.
Douglass executors. Dec. 3, 1826. Proved Feb. 1828. (P.83)

Will of Robert BOYLS - Wife Elizabeth Boyls, one third land and
other property. My son James R. Boyls 100 acres land including house
and etc. One third moveable property. To daughter Nancy Bradford 60
acres. Appoints son James R. executor. Aug. 20, 1813. (P.84)

James RANKIN will - Wife Hannah Rankin one third of tract I live
on stock, etc. To wife land in Kentucky. A bond on Maj. Morehead of
Ky. Daughter Ann Rodget. To John Rankin. To 'Wm. Rankin $10. To
John Blakemore a negro etc. To James Rankin, negroes and to Cage Hale
negroes and money. To Jesse Rankin negro and money. My other children
Caty, Roark, Elizabeth Green, Mary Routon, Sarah Palmer. Wife Susannah.
Had land 180 acres on which I live to James Williams and Jesse Rankin.
Exec. Hannah my wife and son John Rankin, executors. Oct. 25, 1827.
(P.85)

Will of John GARDNER - Wife Mourning land and plantation and
Mansion house we live in etc. My son Cullen Gardner and Sally House
their husband tract land. My daughter Sally House. Appoints Elijah
Roddie and Josiah Howell executors. 15 Jan 1828. Proved 1828. (P.86)

Will of James RANKIN (Relation to J. RANKIN not stated in the will;
To John Rankin. John Blakemore. To James Rankin. To Cage Hale. To
Jesse Rankin.) Wife Hannah to have land. Daughter Ann Fodget. Other
children Caty, Roark, Elizabeth Green, Mary Routon, Sarah Palmer,
Susanna Long. Dated Oct. 25, 1827. Probated Feb. 1828. (P.86)

Will of John GARDNER - Wife Mourning land, and Mansion. Son
Cullen. Child. Sally House. Sarah Wilsey and her children. (P.87)

Will of John THURMOND - Wife Nancy. Mrs. Gregory (NOTE: kin to
wife) Fleming G. Thurmond. John G. Thurmond. Polly Bailey. Frances
Mills. Mary Jane (by last wife.) 1824/6 (This family has been
compiled by Edythe Whitley, traced to 1704, Va., and gives descendants.)

Joseph YOUNG, deceased will - Non-cupative will. By Elizabeth H.
Young & Nicholas Hale & Mrs. M. Young. 8 May 1828. Property sold for
benefit of my children. Proved May 1828. (P.90)

James Sanders executor of Alanson TRIGG, deceased, with Lucy Trigg
executrix. Appeared in court and Qualified. (P.90)

William SANDERS will - To 3 sons Edwin, William and Francis
Pleasant. Lots in Gallatin. Three daughters. Daughters Harriett
Matilda, Dau. Mina John, Octavia, Dethiah. 30 Oct. 1828. (P.90)

James FRANKLIN Sr. will - Son John. Son Isaac. Land Station
Camp Creek. Line of James Franklin Jr. Son James. Son William
Daughter Ann Wood and Betsy. Franklin. Granddaughter Polly Purvis.
Daus. Jane Wood, Ann Wood. Sally Gardner, Betsy Franklin. Son Albert
C. Franklin. Grandson Isaac Purvis. Appoints son James Franklin &
Son-in-law John Wood Exec. Dec. 10, 1828. Proved 1830. (P.91/2)

Richard BLYTHE will - Four sons Elinezer (probably should be
Ebenezer as shown later in will), Richard A. William and Samuel. Mentions
gift from their grandmother Elizabeth Blythe. Children James, Ebenezer,

Richard A., William A., Samuel C., Elizabeth K., Andrew T. and
David M. Blythe. My brothers Andrew Blythe and Samuel K. Blythe,
my father-in-law Wm.C. Alexander and friends Richard King & Thomas
Anderson executors. 5 July 1828. Proved Aug. 1828. (P.93)

John KIRKPATRICK will - Wife Sarah. Two children Isabella
and Martha Jane, and John Rufus. Oct. 18, 1828. Proved Nov. 1828.
(P.94)

James BENTLEY will - Wife Elizabeth land, ferry road. Son-
in-law Reuben M. Blakemore and wife Elizabeth. To daughter Polly
negro. Children: Jeremiah, John, David, Patsy, Emeline, James,
Maud, Nancy S. Bentley. Sons and daughters of mine. Son David
and James M. Jan. 15, 1828. Proved Feb. 1829. (P.95)

John KIRKPATRICK will - Wife Sarah land. Children not all
of age. Two children Isabella and Martha Jane, and John Rufus.
Peter Ritring executor. Proved Nov. 1828. Witnesses, James
Kirkpatrick and Hugh Kirkpatrick. 18 Oct. 1828. (P.95)

James BENTLEY will - Wife Elizabeth the lower end of land I
live on. From the Ferry Road downwards. Son-in-law Reuben M.
Blackemore and wife Elizabeth $5.00. Sons and daughters Polly,
Jeremiah, John, David, Patsey, Meline, James, Maud, Nancy S.
Bentley. Sons David and James M. a horse apiece. My grand-
children sons and daughters of my daughter Elizabeth Blakemore.
Appoints wife Elizabeth and Wm. Bentley executors. 15 Jan.
1828. Proved Feb. 1829. Witnesses: J.L.Swaney, Jeremiah
Bentley, Jonathan Badgett Jr. (P.95)

Joseph WALDRUM will - Wife Amy dwelling house and build-
ings and one third of land I live on. Daughter Patsy lives
with her mother. Son Joseph. Son William. Son John.
Daughter Polly Shearon $1.00. Son Littleton. Daughter Amy
Easley. Daughter Jumy M. Waldrum. Daughter Patsey Waldrum,
tract of land on Tramel Creek. Daughter Becky. Appoints
Samuel Davis, executor. 15 July 1826. Proved Feb. 1829. (P.96)

Mourning GARDNER will - Son Callen Gardner. Daughter Sally
Roan. Grandson John House. Granddaughter Mary Roan. Grand-
daughter Malvina Road (Roan). Two children Callen Gardner and
Sally Roan. Son-in-law Wm. Roan (Hoan) executor. 27 June 1828.
Proved Aug. 1828. (P.97)

Agnes KEESE will - Had a carriage. To George H. Sanders a
cart and farm tool. To May Sanders H.H.Goods. To Redmond Bell
a desk etc. To Jane Ball Household Goods. To Roady Bell (or
Ball). To Champers Ball. To Thomas Keesee $1.00. To George F.
Keesee $1.00. To Champers Keesee $1.00. To Louisa Smith $1.00.
To Patrick Smith $1.00. To Rody McKnight $1.00. To Agnes
Lyning $1.00. To Robert Sanders $1.00. To Nancy Henry $1.00.
Appoints George W. Sanders & James Ball, executors. 10 Feb.
1829. Proved May 1829. (P.98)

48

James ODOM will - Eldest daughter Elizabeth Eliston. To my three grandchildren Jordan Tarren, James Tarren, and Bird Tarren my land where their father Benjamine Tarren now lives on east side Desha's Creek, their mother Sally Tarren to possess her life. To granddaughter Eliza Tarren slave. Son Moses Odom. Daughter Polly Elliott. Granddaughter Betsy Elliott. Son Eli Odom land on Desha Creek.on the west side. Youngest son Harris Odom tract land I live on 290 acres. Son-in-law George Elliott. My daughter Sally Tarren. 16 Feby. 1818. Proved May 1829. (P.99)

Hardy HUNT will - Wife Sally her life certain property. To Hardy H. Seawell $50.00. I give to Martha Jane and Walker Allen $25.00. To Penjamin Page Seawell. To Sally Rowlings. Daughter Elizabeth Mitchell. Daughter Licueritta Stroud. Daughter Penelope Grimsley. Daughter Saorina White. Codicil. Mentions Fielding Grimsley a gift as his wife's. To Patsy Linkey of North Carolina. Appoints Sons Sion Hunt and Thomas Hunt executors. 23 March 1821. Codicil March 1829. March 20, 1839. Proved May 1829. (P.100)

Elisha W. GRAY will - Divide among my brothers and sisters. Appoints John McGee and Wm. L. Alexander executors. 8 July 1829. Proved August 1829. (P.101)

Jonathan PIERCE will - Mother Kaven H. Pierce. Mentions to pay Dr. Richmond for my professional education. Brother Owen Pierce. Appoints Samuel D. Read executor. 1 June 1829. Proved August 1829. (P.102)

William A. TYREE will - Mother Mary Tyree. My brothers and sisters, Sarah C. Stratton, John P. Abraham, Richard C., Mary L., Martha A.B., and Jane C. Tyree. Appoints Brother and Mary Tyree exec. and my brother-in-law Edward Stratton executors. 21 Oct. 1829. Proved November 1829. (P.103)

Abraham TRIBBLE will - Wife Polly. Sons Hezekiah and Elizabeth, Nelson Tribble. Abraham Tribble equal. 15 June 1829. Proved Nov. 1829. (P.103)

Stephen BEASLEY will - Wife Patsy. Appoints Benjamine Charless and Anthony Cotton executors. 21 Aug. 1829. Proved November 1829. (P.104)

James WHITWORTH will - Wife Ann. Daughter Eliza. Daughter Polly. Daughter Elizabeth. Son William. Son James. Daughter Ann. Son Marquis. Daughter Virginia. Daughter Tabitha. Son John. All children not of age. Appoints wife Ann and Jeremiah Stark executors. April 17, 1829. Proved November 1829. (P.104)

Hubbard SANDERS will - Wife Chloe tract land I live on called Clary Tract. Son Thomas not of age. Son Hubbard tract land. Children not all of age namely, Minerva Sanders, William R. Sanders. Tabitha T. Sanders. Catherine M.J.Sanders. Adaline Sanders, Hubbard Sanders. Son-in-law Robert Harper. Son-in-law John A. Walker. Daughter Elizabeth Walker. Son-in-law James M. Gray and my daughter Mariah R. Gray. Son-in-law Peter Bysor and my daughter Sally Bysor. Son-in-law Samuel D. Reed and my daughter Clara Read. Son-in-law Alexander Ewing and my

daughter Chloe Ewing. Son William R. land I bought of Dr. Wagon on
called Davis place, lying on both sides Nashville Road 279 acres
"Stud Horses Comandore Perry and Partnership". Land in Kentucky
and land in Giles Co, Tenn, mentioned. 13 children, Nancy Harper,
Elizabeth Walker, Mariah R. Gray, Sally Rysor, Clarisa Road.
Cole R. Ewing, Manirva Sanders, Catherine M.J.Sanders, and Hubbard
Sanders. Appoints wife Chloe and son-in-law. Samuel D. Read
executors. 5 July 1627. Proved Nov. 1829. (P.105)

Andrew BLYTHE will. - Land on Sith fork in Smith County, Tenn.
Son Samuel M. 1/3 land Desha Creek he lived on. Daughter
Elizabeth land. Son James D. 1/3 land. Son William. Son
Andrew 1/3 land. Wife Martha house etc. Executors Joseph Robb
and my son Samuel M. Blythe and Samuel K. Blythe executors.
4 Nov. 1829. Proved Feb. 1830. (P.108)

Sophia GILLESPIE will - To Nancy Harvey my interest in
$5000. At her death of Jesse Cage's children. To Robert Gillespie
$200. To Allen. To Jesse Cage and his children. Appoints Jesse
Cage executor. 24 Dec. 1329. Proved Feb. 1830. (P.109)

William ALDERSON will - Son John land I live on 250 acres.
Daughter Elizabeth. Daughter Ann. Son William. 5 children,
John Boyle, Wm. Alderson, Annie Harris, Joice Lovel, Elizabeth
Alderson. Appoints Son William and John Royle exec. Oct. 17,
1829. Proved Feb. 1830. (P.110)

William ROBB Sr. will - (Noncupative will) Sons William and
Joseph, property. Daughter Jane Holly. 30 Dec 1829. Pvd. Feb.
1830. (P.110)

Mary RICKMAN will - Son Samuel. Son Robert. Daughter Sally
Owen. Son Samuel. Daughter Elizabeth Stovall. Four daughters
Elizabeth Stovall, Nancy Carter, Fanny Martin and Rebecca Stovall.
Son Samuel Rickman and my daughter. Sally Owen executors.
23 Aug. 1829. Proved Nov. 1829. (P.112)

Amy PECK will - 6 July 1818 - Sister Mary Angan executor,
and James McKendren. Proved Nov. 1829. (P.113)

Francis WITHERS (WEATHERED) - Son John and son Robert land
near creek runs through the Grimfield plantation into Bledsoe
Creek. Son Francis Marcus Wethered 50 acres. Son Thomas
Weathered 50 acres. Son James 38 acres. Son William 50 acres.
Wife Frances dower. Daughter Elizabeth $\frac{1}{4}$. Daughter Milly now
Milly Bledsoe. Daughter Sarah Myers. Son Robert. Appoints
General James Winchester and General Wm. all executors.
22 Jan. 1824. Proved Nov. 1830. (P.113)

Moses BURLEY will - Wife Mary. Children not all by name.
Daughter Mary Cobb. Daughter Sarah Martin. Sons James and
Charles. 15 Aug. 1830. Proved Nov. 1830. (P.115)

William BUSBY will - Wife Elizabeth land. Son John. Daughter Mary. Daughter Martha Tyler. Son Howell. Have given

legacies to John Busby and Mary and Martha Tylor. My children, Harrell, James Lilah, Benjamin, Caroline, William., Samuel Busby. Children to be educated. 27 Sept. 1830. Proved Nov. 1830. (P.116)

Silby HARNEY will - Wife Laurauah. Son Thomas $\frac{1}{2}$ my schooner "Ralley". Son Lemuel $\frac{1}{2}$ my schooner "Ralley". Daughter Laurauah Mercer. Son Benjamin. Sons, Mills, Silby, William and Harney. My nephew Gonethan Harney 100 acres in Tenn. Mentions land give me for my Military service. To Nancy Harney 400 acres in Tenn. My Jumper Swamps to be sold. My sailing boat. Sons, Thomas, Benjamine, Lemuel, Mills, Silby, and William. My brother Thomas Harney exec. 9 April 1800. Codicil 27 Oct. 1800 son Penjamine. Proved Camden County, North Carolina 1801. Some of land in Sumner and some in Smith and some in Jackson Counties in Tenn. Signed Selby Harney. (P.117)

Caren Happuck PEARCE will - Divide between Owen and Caronhappuck Pearce. Daughter Elizabeth Wilson to school her children Sarah M. Wilson. My legatees Kitterah Harper, George Pearce, Isaac Pearce, Henry Pearce, Kizziah Bandy, Elizabeth Wilson. Sally Smith and Harriet Bandy. Son Owen Pearce executor. 25 March 1830. Proved November 1830. (P.119)

James STRODE will - Daughter Polly Clarkson. Son John. Daughter Elizabeth Kerr. Daughter Susan Thomas. Daughter Catherine Bush. Daughter Margaret Wilson. Son William. Son James. Son Charles E. Wife Margaret. Two sons John and William executors. 20 July 1827. Proved May 1830. (P.120)

Owen SULLIVAN will - Son Joseph. Son Isaac. Daughter Sarry. Son Owen 25 acres. Owned land including Nob Spring. Daughter Polly Stenson. Sons Isaac and Joseph youngest sons. A piece of money coming to me from Samuel Wilson. All my children and Sary my wife, Rachel and Samuel, Daniel, James, Polly, Owen, Joseph, Isaac and Saray and Samuel. 21 Dec. 1829. Proved Feby. 1830. (P.121)

Andrew WEST will - Wife Trepluna. Daughter Hannah and her husband Jacob Meadow. Son Thomas West. Daughter Sally. Daughter Phely and her heirs Lewis Hunter. Daughter Rachel and her husband John M. Taylor. Son Daniel. Daughter Phebe and her husband Lewis Hunter. Proved May 1830 (P.122)

John HUDSON will - Son John. Son Benjamine not 21. Wife Mary. Sell lands. Children: Nancy Hudson, John Hudson, Benjamine Hudson, Polly Hudson, Elizabeth Hudson, Sally Hudson, Eliza Hudson, James Hudson, Eli Hudson, Thomas Hudson, Martha Catherine Hudson. 21 Jan. 1830. Proved August 1830. (P.123)

William GLOVER will - Land in Sumner County on Cumberland River 250 acres adjoining Col. Geo. Smith. Auslam D. Bugg and Edw. Sanders deceased. And other land adjoining Joseph Parish, Robert Bell. Mentions interest he has under will of Joseph Motherall which land in Hickman County on both sides Duck River. My sister-in-law Elizabeth Merry to occupy the place. Three sons Edmond, Joseph M., and James Glover. Three friends and brother-in-law Joseph Robb, Joell Parrish and Robert Hodge executors. 1 July 1830. Proved Aug. 1833. (P.124)

John CRABB will - Son Knight Crabb tract land 25 acres.
Division between Susannah More, Precilar Crabb, and Nancy Cangan.
Appoints James Strother and Eliza Busby executors. Proved Jan.
2, 1828. (P.125)

James HARRISON will - Son James plantation I live on. Son
George. Grandson Nathaniel Pladlove Harrison. My other children
Polly Hendon, Massey Williams, Nathaniel Harrison, Susan McKisick,
Rhody Wynne, and Catherine Carr. Son Harry. Daughter Catey
Howel. Appoints my trustees Wm. Hall and son James Harrison
exec. 31 July 1830. Proved Aug. 1830. (P.125)

William ALEXANDER will - Advance age. My good old compan-
ion Mary Alexander. Grandson Richard B. Alexander. Grandson
William the tanner. Granddaughter Tabitha Lawson. Grandson
Richard and William the tanner. Son William Locke Alexander.
Son Wm. L. Alexander executor. Proved Aug. 1830. (P.126)

James BALL will - To Jane and Fanny Ball heirs of my boby.
To James Ball, Isaac Wilson Ball, Richard Ball, and Abner Ball,
heirs of Agnes Jones, Elizabeth Jones, Rebecca Stewarts.
Appoints Isaac Ball and James Carr executors. 22 May 1821.
Proved 1830. (P.127)

David VANCE will - Wife Elizabeth. All my children not
by name. Son John executor. 17 July 1830. Proved Feb. 1831.
(P.128)

James CARR will - Wife Amy land. Son John. Two youngest
sons Jocaman and Jefferson, William Carroll Carr; Children
Jason, John, Jordan, Lancy, Jacannon, Annia, Matilda, Elizabeth,
Jefferson, William Carroll and Sarah Isabella. Appoints Exec-
utor John Carr and Jordon Carr. 28 May 1830. Proved Feb 1831.
(P.128)

Sarah BAYNES will - Daughter Harriett T. Division
between John Haynes, Nancy Jones, Felix G. Haynes, and Elizabeth
Payne. Son Hugh. Son John D. Daughter Nancy P. Jones. Son
Feliz G. Daughter Eliza A. Payne. 24 Oct. 1830. Proved Feb.
1831. (P.129)

Thomas HUNT will - To Chambrose Duffer to him if he stays
with wife. I will him if he stays until age 21 years. My wife
Mary Hunt. Three children Susan Hunt, Sarah A. Hunt. John T.
Hunt. Appoints wife and Stephen R. Gilliam exec. 13 May 1827.
(P.131)

Elijah ROBERTSON will - 13 Nov. 1830. Had a cotton gin.
Wife Nancy. My children not by name. Brother David Robertson
and friend Wm. Carr executors. Proved Feb. 1831. (P.131)

Robert SHAW will - Wife Elizabeth plantation. Son William
Eldest son Thomas $325. Daughter Sarah Stewart. Daughter Jonny
Patterson. Appoints son William and Daniel Lattimer executors.
July 7, 1823. Proved Feb. 1831. (P.132)

Catherine BENNETT - 26 Feb. 1826 will - To Nancy Mucklerath my curtain bed stead. Property divided between Polly Chapman, Elizabeth Jennings, Patsy Sheperd, Clarissa Vinson, Catherine Vinson and Nancy Mucklerath. Appoints Joel Parrish executor. Proved Feb. 1831. (P.133)

Sarah CAMP will - 9 Oct. 1828 - To daughter Nancy Camp land. Granddaughter Rebecca Basil. Daughter Polly Hall. To William Walton. Daughter Patsy Lane. Granddaughter Evaline Hall, Malvira Hall. Wm. Walton executor. Proved Feby. 1831. (P.134)

Robert STEELE will - Daughter Isabel. Son William. Son George. One fourth to 'm. Lyons and Peggy Lyons equally. 9 Dec. 1828. Proved May 1831. (P.134)

Nathan Edwards will - Daughter Priscilla. Sons James and Littleberry. Daughter Sally Hassell. My son William. Son Thomas C. Daughter Patience. Daughter Lovey Cotton. 1 June 1826. Proved May 1831. (P.135)

William KIRK will - 3 single daughters Lucy, Margaret, and Sarah 45 acres land. 4 youngest sons Benjamine, Hezekiah, Robert and Isaac 60 acres land. Appoints son Benjamin executor. 22 Nov. 1830. Proved May 1831. (P.136)

James B. KING will - Land I purchased of Samuel K. Blythe Esqr. be sold. Land in Wilson Co. deeded by Bartholomew. Figures which is in possession of Samuel Calhoun be received by father Richard King. My wife Elizabeth property from her father. Child or children unborn. Brother Robert A. King. 27 May 1831. (P.137)

William BRADFORD will - Wife Nancy. Son ___? Bradford. Proved Aug. 1831. Appoints wife and Prestley Bradford exec. (P.139)

Hugh BARR will - 31 July 1826. Wife Elizabeth. Brother Patrick title to land I give my nephews Wm. Alison and Andrew Allison and James Allison. Rest divided 3 parts to James Barr's sons John and Patrick. Appoints Wm. Barr and Westy Guthrey exec. Proved Aug. 1831. (P.139)

Jesse ROBERTSON will - Wife Susannah. Heirs David, Mildred, Mary, Elijah, Susannah, and heirs of my dead son Elisha. Appoints sons David and Elijah exec. 7 Jan. 1830. Proved Aug. 1831. (P.140)

David CRENSHAW will - Wife Frances. Children equally divided not by name. Wife Frances executor. 19 Oct. 1806. Proved Aug. 1831. (P.141)

James BOYLES will - Estate to be sold. Son-in-law Joseph McGlothlin Brother John. Granddaughters Minerva and Lydia Boyle. Mentions agreement between myself and Levey C. Shy, Rachel Shy (or Sly), into and deposited with Wm. Brackin for safe keeping until called for by parties. My children, Ann McGlothlin, Racheal House, Polly House, Susannah Freedle, and Sinai House. James House heirs of my daughter Sinai Shy. Appoints Joseph McClothlin and Wm. House executors. 8 Oct. 1831. Witness Wm. Brackin and E.J.Brackin. (P.141)

Robert W. BLEDSOE will - Daughter Polly Ann Shoulders, Clarissa and Mildred. Nephew Abraham son of David L. Bledsoe Brother James W. Bledsoe. Brother Anthony T. Bledsoe. Brother David L. Bledsoe. Oct. 11, 1831. (P.142)

John RAGSDALE will - Mother Jane Ragsdale all property. Robert M. Potts to attend collections. Brother Benj. Ragsdale. Jan. 28, 1832. Proved Feby. 1832. (P.143)

John BRESSIE will - Wife Elizabeth. Children mentioned but not by name. 10 Oct. 1831. Proved Feb. 1831.(P.144)

Luke PERDUE will - Wife Susanna. My children not by name. Sept. 5, 1831. Proved Feb. 1832. (P.144)

Edward DOUGLASS now of Wilson County, Tenn. will - Wife Elizabeth. To Elmore Douglass my son. To Norville Douglass my son land. To Wm. A. Douglass my son. Daughter Patsy Hall. Son-in-law Charles E. Sanders and wife Eliza. Daughter Patsy Hall and ____ G. Sanders. Appoints son Harry L. Douglass exec. 16 Jan. 1825. Proved May 1825. (P.145)

Orran (Owen) PEARCE will. Plantation I got from Brother Jonathan's estate. Sarah Ann Wilson infant daughter of my sister Elizabeth Wilson. Joseph P. Wilson father of said Sarah Ann Wilson. My sister Elizabeth Wilson. Appoints Samuel D. Reed exec. 7 Feby 1832. Proved May 1832. (P.146)

Nancy MITCHELL will - 4 Feby. 1832. To Silas Polk my son. To my daughter Jane Williams. To my daughter Amelia Brashiers. To Athena Moore my daughter. Son Hiram Mitchell. Daughter Lucilla Polk. Five children Silas, Jane, Amelia, Anthony and Hiram and my daughter Lucilla. Proved May 1832. (P.147)

John HAMILTON will - Adopted son James Hamilton. My daughter Celia Walker. My son Franklin Hamilton. My son Colney Hamilton. Appoints Fielding N. Blakemore exec. 5 Jan. 1830. Proved May 1832. (P.148)

Edward FERGUSON will - Wife Elizabeth house etc. Children Lucy Green, Tildy Woodruff, Nelson Ferguson. Rebecca Fuller, Nancy Calaway, John Ferguson, Jordan Ferguson, Elizabeth Ferguson, Ann Ferguson. Appoints wife exec. 6 Dec. 1826. Proved Aug. 1832.

Thomas BLAKEMORE will - Son Albert G. Blakemore. Son George W. Blakemore. To Sena. To daughter Matilda Hart. Son Wesley. Son Reuben M. Son Fieldin N. Granddaughter Sarah Taylor. Granddaughter Eliza P. Taylor and Martha A. Taylor. Granddaughter Sena A. Taylor. Granddaughter Sarah E. Blakemore. Son Lee C. Son James. Daughter Elizabeth Dickeson. Son John D. Son Edmond. Appoints son Westly, George W. and Albert G. executors. 21 Jan 1831. Proved Aug. 1832. (P.150)

Mary SEAWELL will - July 21, 1821 - Son Jeremiah Page Seawell.
Son Robert Hicks Seawell. Daughter Martha Thomas Sewell. Daughter
Elizabeth F. Seawell. Proved Nov. 1832. (P.151)

Reuben DOUGLAS will - Wife Elizabeth. Son William J. Daughter
Evaline Franklin wife of Wm. Franklin. Five single daughters Sophia,
Malina, Patsey, Emma and Eliz. Son Willie J. Son Bennet E. Owned
much property. 3 young children my deceased daughter Peggy Green
(Sophia, Edward and Peggy). April 10, 1830. Proved Nov. 1832. (P.152)

Zachariah TALLEY will - Son Wm. P. Tally of Cumberland Co, Va.
Gave him before I left Virginia. Son Jackey Talley of Cumberland Co,
Va. I gave him before I left Virginia. Daughter Charity Talley she
moved to this county. Daughter Lucy Butterworth. Granddaughter Polly
Tally dau. of Charity Tally. Granddaughter Sally Talley. Granddaughter
Lucy M. Talley. Granddaughter Eliza W. Talley. Granddaughter Peomly W.
Talley. Appoints son Zachariah and Reuben Talley executors. 19 April
1820. Proved Aug. 1832. (P.154)

Hiram LEWIS will - Wife Aggy. 10 children. Elizabeth Lewis,
Joshua Lewis, Edmond Lewis, Walton Lewis, David Lewis, John, Lucy,
Pomela and Mary Lewis, Rachel C. Lewis. Appoints Daniel Carney and
Shelton Carney executors. 7 Dec. 1826. Son Hiram W. born since will
written. Proved. (P.155)

Daniel BENDER will - Son Burrell. Son Purdine. Son Burnice.
Son Bryant. Daughter Elizabeth Brooke. Daughter Nancy McColough. Wife
Fereby. Grandson Daniel Feelwood (dissipated). 20 Nov. 1832. Proved
Feb. 1833. (P.156)

Charles IRBY will - Wife Jemima. Son William W. Isley. To Mary
and Eastern Isby (or Irby) each. To Rebecca and Charles S. Irby. To
Susanna and John R. Irby. Children Eastin, Charles, John, Mary,
Rebecca, Sisanna. 26 Dec. 1832. Proved Feb. 1833. (P.157)

William STEWART will - Wife Nancy. Son William Jr. 18 March
1833. Proved May 1833. (P.157)

Joseph WILSON will - Wife Sarah. Daughter Polly Wilson. Daughter
Sarah Barham. Daughter Fanny Barham. Son James T. Daughters Elinor
Elizabeth and Anne. Sons James T. Moses and Montillion W. Wilson. Feb.
9, 1833. May 1833. (P.158)

King CARR will - Appoints Wm. P. and Andrew M. Carr exec. Wife
Elizabeth. Sons William, John and David. 14 March 1833. Proved May
1833. (P.159)

John DALTON will - Son John $290. and tract land I live on Grandson
Tyree son of John Dalton. To Matilda Calty (Catty). Walton Dalton. To
Shelton Dalton. To James Dalton. Sons John and Booker Dalton executors
4 Jan. 1832. Proved May 1833. (P.159)

James HANNA will - Wife Susanna. Sons James Bryson and Abner Lea
tract land purchased of Andrew Rule. Son James Bryson. Son John Doak.
Daughter Patsy Carr land I purchased of Jacob Gillespie and his wife

Amelia. Daughter Lucinda Woodson. Daughter Minerva Tison. Daughter Yettura 80 acres I live on. Her sister Minerva and Tunion (?). 26 March 1833. Proved May 1833. (P.161)

Malissa DOUGLAS will - Mother Elizabeth Douglass. Nephew Wm. Green. Brother William J. and Bennett E. Douglas Exec. 18 June 1833. Proved 1833. (P.162)

Dr. Thomas ESSEX will - Wife Mildred M. I paid immediately after our marriage. Interest 1 Feb. 1829. Son James C. Son Thomas W. had wood factory. Daughter Elmor. Daughter Sarah. Daughter Elizabeth. Grandson John T. Bell. Daughter Ann Hougham. Daughter Elizabeth Bell to her negroes at Cairo. Owned lot in old Fields at Cairo, which we entered for occupancy. Elizabeth's children John T, Lucy Ann and Mildred Bell. Daughter Elmor Mitchell. Appoints Thomas Anderson esqr. and Wm. Montgomery Esqr. exec. 5 July 1832. Proved Aug. 1833. (P.163)

Jamuma B: HODGES will - Five daughters Polly Anderson, Elizabeth Hodges, Sarah M. Hodges, and Mailmda L. Hodges, and Jermina Hodges. 11 Nov. 1833. (P.165)

Jane VINSON will - Children and heir of my daughter Louisiana Bacard. Son James Vinson. James Vinson and exec. of Capt. Vinson. 3 July 1833. Proved Nov. 1833. (P.166)

Leonard BROWN will - Daughter Eleanor Dorris. Daughter Elizabeth Rickman. Son William Brown. Son Thomas Brown. Son Robert Brown. Daughter Susanna Melton (husband John Melton or Milton). Son Robert. 2 Aug. 1824. Daughter Sally Asken. Son Leonard. Daughter Polly Cusbrook (Ausbrook). Appoints Robert Brown and Wm. Dorris exec. Aug. 8, 1828. Proved 1833. (P.166)

Bailey TURNER will - Son William. Son John E. Daughter Jane H. Williams. Daughter Elizabeth Jones. Grandson George T. Fielks children of my daughter Mary F. Fielks. Property to Jane H. Williams, Wm. Turner, George T. Fielks, and child of Elizabeth Jones. 23 Oct. 1833. Proved Feb. 1834. (P.168)

William KEY will - Wife Elizabeth tract land purchased from Wm. Durham. Son William Jr. Heirs of Sally Duncan deceased, Daughter Harruit Key live with her mother. My brother Bingham Key and his wife Sausan. My son Ruffin. My son Alfred C. Grandson Elisha Key son of Thomas. My daughter ? Henry. Daughter Nancy Davis. My son Patterson W. Key. Appoints son-in-law Ruffin Key, Patterson W. Key, Jane Key and Moses H. Henry exec. 24 Dec. 1833. Proved. (P.169)

George W. RAWLINGS will - Wife Mary. Friend Bartholomew Watkins. Nephew Benjamine R. Howard. Sister Burnetta E. Rawlings land deeded to me by my father Benjamin Rawlings. Brother Rufus K. 4 Nov. 1833. (P.172)

Robert LAWRENCE will - Stepson Henry H. Daugherty. Benj. Gaines son of Patsy Gaines wife of Thomas Gaines. To Nancy Gaines daughter of Patsy Gaines wife of Thomas Agines. To Alfred Gaines son of Patsy Gaines wife of Thoms. Gaines. 13 Sept. 1828. (P.173)

William BRACKIN will - Wife land I live on 340 acres. Sons Elvis J. negroes. Son James L. Daughter Eliza B. Daughter Elvira and her husband Samuel Turner. Brother-in-law Reuben Searcy and his wife Polly. 3 April 1833. (P.174)

Will of William BRACKIN - Wife Plantation I live on 340 acres. Son Elvis J. Brackin. Son James L. Brackin. Daughter Eliza B. Brackin. Daughter Elvira her husband Samuel Turner. My brother-in-law Reuben Searcy and his wife Polly. 30 April 1833. (P.174)

Will of Henry BOOTH - Tract land purchased of Mrs. Buckner, to be sold. My three children Elizabeth, James and John not of age. My brother William to have management of my daughter and her property until she marries, also of my two boys. Appoints Coo R. Dismukes and Wm. Booth executors. 1833-4. (P.175)

Elizabeth BARNES will - Two sons Matthew I. Jones and Albert C. Franklin. Owned land 13 Jan. 1834. (P.176)

Will of John PEYTON Sr. 3 youngest children namely, Rebecca H. Parker, Joseph H. Peyton, Sally H. Peyton. Other children not by name. Owned little piece of land near Thomas Keefe sold to son Palio Peyton. Mentions case of McKoin against me lately in Nashville. I owe the administrators of Elmore Douglas out of some land. Mentions land I live on. Sept. 1, 1833. (P.176)

Drury SCRUGGS will - Children Drury, and Gross Scruggs and Elizabeth Hoody. Grandson Felix Buckles. Appoints Enoch P. Connell and Isaac Walton executors. 7 August 1833. (P.176)

Will of William DORRIS - July 31, 1829. Wife Katherine my land. (P.177)

Will of Simon PRESCOTT - Wife Polly all estate. 12 Oct. 1833. Her death divide among children. Children: my two little children Allvin Prescott and Tabitha Prescott. Proved 1833. (P.178)

STEAMBOAT, TENNESSEE. - Jan. 16, 1833. - Will of JOHN H. SMITH Jr. Death may come at any time. Wife Melvina D. Mentions papers and provisions in the papers in the estate of George Smith decd in the name of W.H.Smith deceased. (P.178)

John SIMPSON - March 7, 1816 will - Wife Elizabeth (R178)

State of Missouri, County of Madison. 13 May 1834, before Wm. M. Newberry clerk of the county court. Appeared Wm. Anthony and Jane Bennett who is identical person with Jane Gilliam. John Simpson died 13 May 1834. (P.179)

57

Richard KING will - 16 April 1834 - Tract land I live on 180 acres is mentioned. To son Robert A. King. To Robert J. King tract land in Wilson County, 48 acres deeded by Bartholomew Firgures to James R. King and by James R. King willed to myself. Robert A. King to sell to settle business certain property. Confirming to heirs and assigns of James R. King deceased right and title to negroes. Granddaughter Martha K. Calhoun not of age. To James Henry King second son of Robert J. King, negroes. To grandson Richard Davis King oldest son of Robert A. King. Granddaughter Elizabeth Sarah King who is the eldest daughter of Robert A. King. Rebecca eldest daughter of Ann about 5 years of age. Grandsons Anderson Tengus and Samuel Calhoun King, youngest son of Robert A. King. Appoints Thomas Anderson and Levi Donnell executors. 1834. (P.179)

Jesse HOLLIS will - Wife to have property her life. Children: Daughter Polly. Son Jesse G. Son John A. Sidney Jane Hollis. Thomas Hollis, Charles W. Hollis. Sarah Margaret Hollis, Elisha Dunhell, Erwin Hollis, Matilda Briganoo Harman Hollis. Melissa Hollis. Appoints Jesse Gambling and Josiah Walton executors. 2 Aug. 1834. Proved Nov. 1834. (P.180)

Nuncupative will of JOHN H. TURNER - 4-5-6 Oct. 1834. At his own dwelling in the town of Gallatin. During last illness of his. If his wife had child, child to have property, etc. His brother S.H.Turner mentioned. His mother Lucy Turner mentioned. Proved Nov. 1834. (P.180)

William CAPPS will - Wife Nancy land three tracts. Son Ridley. Son Ewington. 19 Oct 1834. Proved 1834 November. (P.181)

Levi HALL will - Son James land I live on adjoining James Murry and Isaac Donoho. Son James. Son Marley land I live on. Two grandchildren Elias Hall and Levi Hall orphan children of my son Samuel Daughter Sally Pitt. Grandchildren heirs of Sally Pitt. Appoints son James Hall executor. 25 March 1832. Proved Nov. 1834. (P.182)

Will of Wm. H. DOUGLASS - My mother. My wife land life which her father left her. All my children. Wife Sally executor and my brother Dr. Elmore Douglass and son Henry L. Douglass exec. My son Henry. My uncle Elmore. My mother not by name. Son not yet 21 years of age. 2 June 1833. (P.182)

Will of Nancy HANNA - Daughter Susannah L. Senter. Son Clifton A. Jones. Land I live on water Bledsoe Creek. Appoints Wash Senter executor. 19 Nov. 1834. Proved Feb. 1835. (P.184)

John ASPLEY will - Wife Sally. Sons and daughters William, John, Samuel, Polly, Patsey, Betsey, Nancy, Sally and Jensey Aspely. Sons William and Samuel executors. Jan. 28, 1821. Proved Feby. 1835. (P.185)

Persis DONNELL will - 6 Oct. 1832. Wife not by name. Property in my father's possession. Educate my children. Son John H.

Donnell. Son Thomas W. Donnell and son Wm. Donnell. Proved Feb. 1835. (P.186)

Will of Thomas WHITE - Wife Cassander. Son mentions to have land I live on and his wife Elizabeth. At their death to Kenelm White Daughter Ally Sears. Son Janeln White. Daughter Mary Buckley. Daughter Elizabeth Patterson. Daughter Mary Brinkley (?). Son-in-law Henry A. Brinkley, executor. July 16, 1830. Proved 1835. (P.186)

Jacob BARHARD will - Son David. Daughter Darcus Atchinson. Daughter Nancy Atchinson. Granddaughter. Nathan Atchinson daughter of Nancy. Daughter Cassander Barnard. Daughter Susannah. Daughter Massey. 26 Oct. 1834. Proved May 1835. (P.187)

Thomas FOXALL - 18 March 1835, Pvd. May Ct. 1835, Will - Wife Mary plantation whereon I now live; 29 acres, impliments - not include 35 acres adjoining which I purchased of Mrs. Elizabeth Barnes on waters of Station Camp Creek. Horses purchased from James Barrow. Mary had "property when I married her". Wife to have slaves; liberates certain slaves. Land purchased of Hill Cryer, the same which the wife of Hudson Thompson has a life interest in. Youngest child of my dec'd brother James Foxall. Brother Richard Foxall. My dec'd brother's children viz. Elizabeth, John, and the infant which the widow was pregrant with at death of my brother. To Richard $100. Appoint Robert Desha exec. Admr. to be guardian for children of James Foxall, dec'd. Wit: John Cryer, Asa Hassell. (P.188)

James RONEY Sr. Will - Nov. 12, 1833. Proved May Court 1835 - Wife Catherine, property, negroes, & at her death to be sold by exec. & divided among - James Roney Jr., Sam Roney, Wm. Roney, John Roney, Elizabeth Dinning, Susannah Graves, Lindy Woodall. The heirs of my deceased daughter Margaret Cage. Granddaughter Susannah House. Appoint son James Roney & my son William Roney and my son-in-law Christopher Woodall as executors. Wit: Henry C. Winbourn, Allen Graves, Abram Bradley. (P.190)

William McKENDREE - 24 January 1833 Will - Proved May Court 1835. Friend Dr. Henry Wilkins of Baltimore County, Maryland, my watch. Two sisters, Dolly Harris, Nancy D. McKendree. Brother James McKendree. To Joshua Soule all my manuscripts & papers to be disposed of as he, with assistance of Thomas L. Douglas may deem most expedient. Land owned in Illinois to the Bishop of the Methodist Episcopal Church in trust; establish literary institute for benefit of the Illinois and Missouri conference. To friend Josh T. Elliston, Esqr, of Davidson Co. my portfolio. To friend M.R.W.Hill of Nashville my blacked cane and silver seal. To friend Elijah Boddie of Sumner Co. Appoints Joshua Soule, James McKendree, Joseph T. Elliston. M(H)R.M(?)Hill & Elijah Boddie, executors. Wit: Elijah Boddie, John Carr, V.W.McKendrie, P.W.Martin. Proved by Harris Odum, Dempsey Ashford, John Carr, James Stratton as securities. (P.191)

Richard ALLEN - 20 March 1835 Will, Proved - Wife Susan, house and plantation whereon I now live except part in Brushey Fork Bottom. Son Davis Allen. Son William Allen land lying westward of line cuts off the plantation, called Davis Field - hill towards Lewis Hunter's hill. Son

Richard Allen. Heirs of my dec'd son John Allen $1.00 etc. Appoints my two sons William & Richard Allen exec. Wit: William Durham, Nath Parker. (P.192)

John TURNER - May 18, 1835 Will. Proved August Court 1835 - Eldest son Nelson R. Turner. Land purchased from Harris Walton. Land on which lives Richard C. Johnston. Land I live on divided between son James and my dau. Sally. To youngest son James land 76 acres bought of James Bledsoe and $\frac{1}{4}$ of land which Richard C. Johnston now lives on. Mentions Brushy Fork, land. Daughter Frances Johnston. Daughter Rebecca Johnston. Daughter Elizabeth Harten. Daughter Eliza Carter. Daughter Mary Ann Henley. Daughter Sally and Son James. Appoint son Nelson R. Turner and William M. Carter exec. Wit: J.A.Blackmore, W.B.Smith, William Durham. (P.192)

Abram STANFIELD will - Wife Mary. Children: Ashley Stanfield, Josiah Stanfield, Mary Stanfield, Mary Willis, Sarah Bowen, Amy Seay, Cinderilla Caldwell, Elizabeth Caldwell, Polly Eilks, Amy Seay. 11 Oct. 1831. (P.194)

William C. CARR will - Wife Mierva Carr. Daughter Sophia Ann. Daughter Elizabeth Carr. May 8, 1835. (P.195)

William SUIT will - Daughter Permelia Suit and her daughter. Francis Elizabeth Elvira. Three children son Bartlett, His son William Jordan Suit not 21 years old. Son Solomon. To Wm. Irsa Suit and on Gallatin Road. 11 July 1833. (P.196)

C. H. DOUGLASS will - Wife Rebecca L. My children. James Scurlock Douglass to be educated as physician. My brother James L. appointed guardian to my son Alex. Augustine Douglas and to my daughter Caroline Louisa Matilda Douglass. My children James Scurlock, Alexander Augustus, Carolinee L., their grandfather James Scurlock deceased. My brother Edward L. Douglas. Mentions Hemp factory business with Stokley D. Vinson. Appoints Isaac Douglas and Young M. Douglass executors. Aug. 28, 1835. Proved 1835. (P.197)

Abram STANFIELD will - Wife Mary. Ashley Stanfield. Josiah Stanfield. Mary Stanfield. Mary Willis. Sarah Bowen. Amy Seay. Cinderilla Caldwell. Elizabeth Caldwell. Polly Wilks, Amy Seay and Elizabeth Caldwel. Appoints Son Josiah Stanfield as Trustee. Daughter Cinderilla Caldwell. Daughter Sally Bowen. Appoints Mary Sanfield, Josiah Stanfield executors. William Seay also exec. 11 Oct. 1831. Proved Aug. 1835. (P.194)

William C. CARR will - Wife Minerva. Daughter Sophia Ann and daughter Elizabeth Carr. Mentions land on Seulers Branch of Bledsoe Creek. My brother John S. and Wilson S. Carr exec. May 8, 1835. Proved Aug. 1835. (P.195)

William SUIT will - Daughter Permilia Suit (her dau. Frances Elizabeth Elvira). My three children. Son Bartlett (his son

Wm. Jordan Suit not 21 years age). Son Solomon Suit. To son Solomon where Wm. Irsa Suit lives. 11 July 1833. Proved Aug. 1835. (P.196)

Will of William C. CARR - May 8, 1835 - Wife Minerva. Daughter Sophia Ann and Daughter Elizabeth Carr. Place I live on Sellers Branch and Bledsoe Creek mentioned. Brothers John S. Carr and Wilson S. Carr. Will proved August 1835. (P.196)

Will of William SUIT - Daughter Permilia Suit. Daughter Francis Elizabeth Elvira, land on North of Gallatin Road including dwelling. Three children. Son Bartlett until his son William Jordan Suit arrives to age 21 years, a tract of land. Son Soloman Suit. Land to William Irsa Suit. Appoints Bartlett Solomon and Permelia and S.H.Turner as executors. July 11, 1833. Proved August 1835 by oath of Wm. Bryley. (P.196)

Will of A. H. DOUGLASS - Wife Rebecca L. Douglass. My children. James Scurlock Douglass a physician. My brother James L. Douglass be guardian to my son Alexander Augustus Douglass. Also to Carolina Louisa, Matilda Douglass. My children's grandfather James Scarlock deceased estate mentioned. My brother Edward L. Douglass mentioned. Mentions having a Hemp factory business with Stokley D. Vinson. James Douglass and Young N. Douglass named executors. 28 August 1835. Proved Nov. 1835. (P.197)

Will of Sarah HUBBERT - To Walter Dickerson for benefit of his mother her life and then to Polly Smith. My nephew Greenville Stone. My niece Polly Smith tract land 50 acres. Appoints Walker Dickerson, Greenville Stone and Perrie Smith as executors. Aug. 13, 1835. Proved Nov. 1835. (P.198)

Will of Rachel (Rachael) LOONEY - Daughter Polly Looney. Daughter Elizabeth Scobey. Granddaughter Caroline Scobey. My daughter Polly Looney and my son Jonathan D. Looney. My two sons Isaac and Edward Looney and Edward C. Looney and my daughter-in-law Caroline Looney. 16 June 1835. Proved Nov. 1835. (P.199)

Will of Thomas KEEFE - Feeble in health. Son Thomas. Wife Margaret and children by name Thomas, Nancy, Martha Jane. Appoints wife Margaret and friend Elijah Roddie, esq., executors. Proved Nov. 1835. (P.200)

Will of John CURRY - Wife Margaret to support family. Land mentioned. My children, Thomas Jefferson, Permelia, Mary Jane, Margaret, William Carrol and Elizabeth Curry. Friend William Curry qualified for heirs. Appoints Wm. Curry and Hugh C. Elliott as executors. 12 July 1835. Proved Nov. 1835. (P.201)

Will of Philman W. WYLLIE - Son Hugh. All right in estate and all dower that my mother Mary V. Wyllie has in her life. If my son Hugh Wyllie dies without lawful heirs, my Brother George A. Wyllie and children. I leave my brother George A. Wyllie as executor and guardian of my son Hugh Wyllie. Son Hugh not 21 years of age. 5 Dec. 1835. Proved Feby. 1836. (P.202)

Will of Henry CLEMEY - Layout property for father and mother.
Appoints friends William C. May and Lewis W. Crunk executors.
3 Dec. 1835. Proved Feby. 1836. (P.202)

Will of Gardner DAVIS - Neice Emily Jackson May $1,000. to be
placed in hands of her father Richard Hillay. She is not 18 years
old. My three neices Sophia Nafe, Caroline Nafe, and Mary Nafe.
My brother Thomas T. Davis. Two brothers Reddin and Thomas T.
Davis. My brother-in-law Richard H. May, and brother Thomas T.
Davis executors. 8 Feby 1836. Proved Feb. 1836. (P.203)

Will of David ORMAND - Daughter Polly. Son Thomas J. "I
give Matilda Johnson fifty dollars on my Family Bible to be
continued in the family" 3 daughters Matilda Johnson, Jane
Johnson, and Polly Ormand equally. My step-daughter Sarah Ann
Wilson to have her mother's bed. Nominate William Chapman and
Robert King as executors. 22 Nov. 1835. Proved Feb. 1836.
(P.204)

Will of John WOOD - Wife Jane. 138 acres land Bledsoe's
Creek. My children. Son Charles. Son Robert $85.00. My
daughter Sarah $85.00. Son William F. $15.00. Appoints son
James F. Wood and John Wood, executors. 24 Oct. 1834. Proved
Feb. 1836. (P.204)

George H. SMITH will - Low state of health. Wife Louisa
B. and children. Children: Calvie James, John and George Ann
Smith. 26 August 1835. Proved Feb. 1836. (P.205)

Will of Nimwood BROWN - Wife Susanna T. Two children
Amanda C. and Reuben B. Brown. 13 Aug. 1835. Proved Feb.
1836. (P.205)

Will of William Smith WEBB - Youngest son William Smith
Webb 260 acres land the place John Armfield lived. Sons and
daughters, Elizabeth Griffith, Samuel Webb, Ann Burnet, Armstead
Webb, Joseph Webb, Nancy Latimer, William Smith Webb. Appoints
Samuel Webb and Armstead Webb as executors. 28 Feby. 1836.
Proved May 1836. (P.206)

Will of William HARPER - Wife and children. Wife Rebecca
Harper land west of creek running near Benj. S. Harper's shop.
To Edmond Harper land he lived on. To son Benj. S. Harper land
he lives on. To Samuel W. Harper land he lives on. To Patty
Parker her part. To General S. Harper my grandson $1250. He
not yet 21 years old. Four children, John Harper, Benj. S.
Harper, and Samuel W. Harper, appointed guardian to General S.
Harper. 14 Feb. 1836. Proved Feb. 1836. (P.207)

Will of Francis MARSHALL (or Frances) - My son David Marshall.
To David Hardaway Jesse and the heirs of Richard Marshall, certain
property. My children 8 others (Nancy, Phebe, Josiah, Francis,
Polly, Rebecca, Elizabeth and Jane). To Partheny and Malena
Marshall. To Melena and Parthena Marshall not 21 yet. Wife
Sarah Marshall. 1835. Proved 1836. (P.208)

Will of Joel BROWN - Eldest son John Brown. Second son Stephen
Brown. Daughter Polly Acrey. Son John Brown. Daughter Peggy Payne.
Daughter Raney Laseter. Appoints Jesse Laseter and John Brown
executors. March 4, 1834. Proved 1835-6. (P.209)

Will of Elisha BARNARD - Wife Rebecca, house and etc. Four dau-
ghters, Susanna Maberry, Lacretia Atchison, Margaret Hendricks and
Rebecca Barnard. Two granddaughters Elizabeth and Lucretia. Sons
William, James, Elisha and Jacob Barnard $1.00 each. Son Luke land I
live on 235 acres. Son Luke and John Hobday executors. March 18, 1836.
Proved August 1836. (P.209)

Will of Robert PATTON - Wife Susanna land. I owe heirs of Daniel
Benthall decd. Son Theophilus Mann Patton tract land I live on 250
acres. Son William Patton. Daughter Genny Watson and my daughter-in-
law Mary Patton remain on place they now live. Appoints friend Joseph
Kirkpatrick and my son Theophilus Mann Patton executors. 15 Sept. 1829.
Proved Aug. court 1830. (P.210)

Note regarding the above will. Samuel Watson and others contested
the will of Robert Patton. (P.211)

Will of Wright BARNES - Feeble. Son Lewis. Daughter Araminta.
Son James. Son Thomas. Wife Nancy and 4 children William, Jane,
(or James), Samuel and Joel. Four oldest children, Elizabeth, Nancy,
Polly and Zachariah, they have received. Appoints Solomon Shoulders
executor. 2 July 1836. Proved Sept. 1836. (P.212)

Will of Samuel ALLEY Sr. - My children, Benjamin Alley, Peter Alley,
Willis Alley, and Molly Kirkham, Lucy Hodges, and Dicy Alley. My grand-
children of my son Samuel Alley decd. by his first wife get equal portions
like my daughter-in-law Allry. My son Joseph Alley. Appoints Joseph
McGlothlin Jr. and Thomas Hamlin executors. 18 Jan 1835. Proved 1836.
Proved by Theophilus Webb and etc. (P.212)

Will of Philip VANCE - Wife Mary land I live on her life. At her
death to divide between her children and my children. Wife and John J.
James, executors. 28 Aug. 1836. Proved. I understand that my brother
David Vance caused to be made to my wife Mary Vance, a deed to the
plantation I now live on for her life. Proved Oct. 1836. (P.213)

Will of John WILSON - Wife Anna. Tract land I live on 50 acres and
dwelling house. Son Samuel. Daughter Sally. Granddaughter Mary Ann
Wilson. Land in Bedford County, Tenn, mentioned. Son James. Daughter
Susan. Granddaughter Mary Ann and gd. Lydia Wilson children of my
daughter Archa deceased, to have tract land on which their father lived
in Bedford County, Tenn, 100 A. Son Samuel and William Walton, esq. to
be executors. Dec. 5, 1833. Proved Nov. 1836. (P.216)

Will of Magdalana MAY - Only daughter Morgan B. May not 18 years
age. My mother and sister Mary A. Wallace to live on my plantation. My
sister Mary A. Wallis. Appointed Brother James Wallace executor.
30 Aug. 1836. Proved 1836. (P.216)

Will of John TURNER, proved. Circuit Court. Will not recorded
here. (P.217)

Will of Spisly C. WINSTON - Wife Minerva E. T. Winston.
Brother Norl C. Winston tract land. My mother Patsy Winston. I
have slave in North Carolina. Deeded to United Baptist Church at
Second Creek, 1 acre of land. Brothers Joseph and Wm. Winston.
Sister Eliza. My wife. Appoints R. S. Coleman, and Noel C.
Winston and my wife Minerva E. T. Winston executors. 22 April
1836. Proved 1837. (P.217)

Will of Edward JONES - Land to children. My sons and my
daughter Elizabeth Savely. Son Gabriel, executor. 12 Feb.
1837. Proved April 1837. (P.219)

Will of Samuel DORRIS - My 'Allie. Wife Abigail. Son
Isiah Dorris land. Son Josiah H. Dorris tract land. Son Josiah
F. Dorris 100 acres. Daughter Eliza Hutson. Daughter Elizabeth
Jackson. Daughter Polly Ford. Daughters, Elizabeth Jackson,
Rebecca Lester, Nancy Edson, Polly Ford, Peggy Edson, Abby Ford,
Milley Olham, and Elizabeth Hudson. March 24, 1837. Proved
April 1837. (P.219)

Will of John BEARDUE (BEARDEN) - Daughter Rebecca Parrish
land she lives on. Three sons, John, Lambert, Smith and Orange
D. (I think Lambert Smith is one name here). Son Solomon's 7
children. Appoints friends Wm. Hall, Charley Morgan and my
son Orange D. executors. 6 July 1837. Proved Sept. 1837. (P.221)

Will of King LUTON - 6 Feb. 1837. Wife Anna. Son King.
Son James. Son Frederick. Son Thomas, Daughter Mary. Son
Charley. Proved Oct. 1837. (P.222) (See my files for this
man's record.)

Will of Henry M. FRANKLIN - Brother Thomas Franklin tract
of land bought of Smith C. Franklin and myself of the estate of
John Franklin deceased. 239 acres and other tracts of land.
A yellow man named Warren owned by Isaac Franklin etc. mentioned.
Brother Thomas J. Franklin have my watch and $125.00. John
Franklin decd. estate and his widow dower right mentioned. John
Lauderson $500. to be paid to his guardian when my estate is
wound up. My brothers and sisters equally, and names as Smith
C. Franklin, Thomas J. Franklin, Martha Armfield, Julia Cage,
John Franklin, Joshua Franklin. Appoints John Armfield and Jesse
Cage as executors. 18 June 1837. Proved October 1837.
(P.222-223)

Will of Richard JONES - 18 May 1827. Going to journey to
Alabama. Have already given my children equal share namely,
Jane Stephens, Polly Hammond, Nancy Jones, Squire Jones, For-
lunathus Jones, Betsy Kizer, Celia Turentine and Cynthia
Richardson. Wife Mary Jones land I live on. Daughter Mahala
Summer Jones. 3 sons William B. Jones, Richard Jones, and
James Buchanan Jones. Appoints Wm. B., Richard and James B.
Jones as executors. Proved Oct. 1837. (P.224)

Will of John DENNING - $10.00 to heirs of Caden Hunter decd
begotten of the body of my daughter Phebe. To Thelma Groves

$10.00. To Richard Smith $10.00. To Henry Williams $10.00 (or $100.).
To George Watwood $100.00. To heirs of Andrew Denning deed $10.00. To
James Mays $150. To William Anderson $150.00. To by deed of gift to
son James Denning some negroes said James not to have property until
after death of John and Polly Denning the father and mother of said
James. Remainder to be equally divided between Henry Williams, William
Alderson, James Mays and William Denning. Appoints Joseph McGlothlin
Jr. and Wm. Lovell as executors. 17 Feb. 1837. Proved Nov. 1837. (P.225)

Will of William PROCTOR - Daughter Elizabeth wife of James Nolan,
$1.00. Daughter Rebecca Pearden wife of John Rearden $1.00. To Sally
Hamlet wife of Thomas Hamlet $1.00. To Polly Pass wife of Gilford Bass
$1.00. To Patsy Parrish wife of Henry Parrish $1.00. My five children
which my last wife bore me, formerly Henoretta Bearding, children by
name, Wm. W., Fannie S. L., Presberry, George W., Joseph F., the
children by my last wife not all of age. Appoints Orange Beardin to
take George and Joseph my two youngest sons to raise and educate. Appoints
James Hosley executor. 10 May 1837. Proved Nov. 1837.

Will of William CUMMINGS - Wife Margaret land and etc. At death
of wife to my five children, James, Moses, Sally, Nancy and Thomas.
Appoints John Cotton, Margaret Cummins my wife and Richard D. Hobday
executor. Nov. 2, 1837. Proved Jan. 1836 (?) (P.227)

Will of Patrick BARR - 4 April 1834. Son William land I live on.
I give to James one half land on which son Robert lived to be laid off.
To Robert one half of land. To Hezekiah and Samuel. Two grandson
John Cowan Barr, and James A. Barr, land their father lived on and
$600.00. Son Hugh $1600. Daughter Mary. Six children: William,
James, Mary, Robert, Hezekiah and Samuel. Sons William and James exec-
utors. Proved June 1838. (P.228)

Will of Samuel D. READ - Wife Clarissa L. Read land and etc. I
desire my executors to pay to John Hardy $230. and send to care of John
Read, Huntsville. Appoints Priestly Bradford and James Howard executors. Proved May 1838. (P.229)

Will of Smith C. FRANKLIN - My two children John Franklin and
James Franklin not of age. Sister Julia Cage. Mentions Thomas J.
Franklin as a brother. Mentions the estate of John Franklin decd.
Appoints Jesse Cage executor. 14 March 1838. Proved May 1838.
(P.229)

Will of James RUTHERFORD - Wife Elizabeth, plantation. My
children. Son Robert. Daughters, Betsy H. Ketrel, Penny C. Hutcherson,
Mary P. Evans, and Minerva L. Taylor. Wm. Rutherford and your two
children, namely, James F. and Elizabeth Cora Rutherford. All my
children, namely - B.L.Rutherford, A.F.Rutherford, T.W.Rutherford,
F.H.Rutherford, Betsy H. Ketrell (Kittrell), P.C.Hutcherson, M.P.Evans,
M.L.Taylor, (B.S.Rutherford, A.T.Rutherford, T(?) W. Rutherford and
F. H. Executors.) Proved May 1838. (P.231)

Will of Richard PARKER - Wife Nancy. Son George W. Parker land
deeded from Wm. Minhaw and etc. Five sons, John, Nathaniel, William,
J. Newton and George W. Parker. Oct. 22, 1831. Proved April 1838. (P.233)

Will of Jane HOWDESTILT - Aughter Jane Howdestelt. Son
Jeremiah. Daughter Sarah. Four daughters Margaret Gray,
Sarah Brown, Jane and Amanda Bowdselt and Jeremiah Howdestelt.
I purchased land of Joseph Howdestelt and Stephen Wilson, it
to Jeremiah. April 16, 1838. Proved June 1838. (P233)

Will of Amy HARGRAVES - Son-in-law Wm. Hutcherson. Four
grandchildren, Mary, William, Martha and Nancy. Daughter Polly
Lanier. 12 Jan. 1834. Appoints Wm. Hutcheson and Robert Lanier,
executors. Proved Jan. 1838. (NOTE: Polly Lanier may be
Polly Jouier or Joiner) (P.234)

Will of Robert HOLMES - March 12, 1833. Sons Thomas
Holmes, and Albert G. Holmes, and Elouis. Wife Margary. March
15, 1833. Signed Robt. Holmes. Proved March 1838. (P.235)

Will of William LAUDERDALE - Wife Hellen plantation I
live on. Land in Gibson County Western District. Children
Mary and John. Children, James H., Sarah H., Samuel W., Mary
P. and John M. Proved 1835. (P.235) (See Lauderdale family
by Whitley)

Will of William MONTGOMERY - Now in 73rd year of age. Wife
Jane (companion and fellow traveler from our youth until now).
We are far advanced in age. Son Daniel $2000. Land in Rutherford
County, Tenn, mentioned. Daughter Margaret M. Bell and her
husband William M. Bell. Daughter Jane Simpson. Daughter
Hannah Nielson. Son John. Son Robert. Land in Robertson
County, Tenn. Son William. Son Jefferson Thomas. Grand-
daughter Mary I.M. and Elizabeth C.W. and Roulston. June 30,
1835. Proved 1838 Oct. Signed Wm. Montgomery. (P.237)

Will of Mearcus ROBERTSON - Wife Margaret Robertson.
Appoints Rouland Horsley executor. 6 Sept. 183_. Proved
Sept. 1838. (P.240)

Will of Skelton SMITH - Wife and children. Wife Jaine C.
Smith land I live on. Daughter Sarah Smith. Daughter Elizabeth.
S. Smith. Daughter Mildred Smith. Granddaughter Elcy B. Smith.
Mentions Bartlett Smith, Rushrod W. Smith, Nathan A. Smith,
Robert Hew Smith (or Robert How), Mecran Smith, Thomas Z. Smith.
March 28, 1838. (P.240)

Will of Mark JUSTIN - Wife Nelly Justin. Daughters Sally
Hail, Anny Pherry. Son Francis Justice. Daughter Rebecca Ray.
Daughter Susan Kirkham. Grandson Addison Justin. Heirs of
Rebecca Ray and Susan Kirkham. Appoints Meredith Hodges and
Nelly Justice exec. April 25, 1832. (P.241)

Will of Richard BASKERVILLE - Wife Elizabeth. Plantation
I live on land on Fledsoe Creek. Four sons: George A. Baskerville, John A. Baskerville, Thomas B. Baskerville and William
Baskerville. Daughter Jane S. Parr. Daughter Eliza Baskerville.
13 July 1838. Proved 1838 Nov. (P.242)

Elizabeth BARR will - June 1, 1838 - 5 equal parts. To Bettie
Foster. To Kitty Johnson. To children of David Foster descendants in
Mason Co, Illinois. (Robert, John C., Ibby, Nancy Betsy, and Wm. Foster,)
Divide between Francois Johnson, Robert W. Guthrie, Nancy Jouthrie,
Betsy Foster, Kitty Johnson. June 1, 1838. (P.244)

Kisiah S. DAVIS - 16 Oct. 1833 will - Feeble, but sound mind.
Beloved husband James P. Davis dec'd. Our graves enclosed. Little
dau. Eliza J. Davis all goods. Dau. Elizabeth Davis, note in hand on
Thomas Shelton; note on Mr. Southall; note on Mr. Perkins; one on Samuel
Winstead; one on William Hanna. My agent Robert P. Cannon of Williamson
Co., Franklin, Tenn. Sister Eliza G. Manning to raise my infant dau.
Eliza J. Davis & she to have $100. annually. My husband's nephew
Sylvester P. Davis $200. Test: John Chambers, I.H.Wilson, C.B.Malone.
Pvd. Deer Court 1838. (P.244)

Lucella GRANGER - 16 May 1838 will - Funeral expenses be paid.
Brother Hiram Mitchell. Sister Jane Williams. Mentions __?__ Moore
and Emily Brashaw. To Emily Branhan. To sister Emily Brandon 50 acres
on which she now lives. To my neice Julia Braham. To enclose my
mother's graveyard. Appoints Hiram Mitchell exec. Wit: J. Harrison,
Wm. M.C.Barr, Eli Marshall. Securities: Meridith Hodges, P.W.Martin.
Pvd. August Court 1838. (P.245)

Mariah LAYAN - 17 July 1834 will - To my aunt Mary Hall $100. To
Dr. N.D.L.F.Sharp $30. To Miss Martha Ann Hall bed etc. To cousin Jane
Scott, saddle etc. To neice Mary Alexander Haynes etc. she not of law-
ful age. To uncle Wm. Hall. Appoint Brother-in-law Felix G. Haynes
executor. Wit: Rachel J. Blackmore, Cathrine D. Barry, Henry Keber.
Securities: John L. Belote, Henry W. Swaney. Pvd. Sept Court 1838.
(P.247)

Elanor PHAGAN - June 7, 1837 will - All debts be paid. Remainder
to daughter Katherine K. Odum. Appoints: Joseph Robb, William H.
Douglass and Alfred H. Douglass executors. Test: Bailie Peyton, Norval
Douglass. Eli Odom was appointed Admr. Pvd. February 1839. (P.247)

William EDWARDS of Town of Gallatin - January 3, 1839 Will -
To William Cantrell $1,000. To Z.P.Cantrell $1,000. To D.H.Cantrell
$1,000. To G.C.Cantrell $1,000. To Sally Willis $500. To L.B.Edwards
$1,000. To Lovey Cotton $500. To Sally Hassell wife of Asa Hassell
$500. To Patience Cotton wife of Hugh Cotton $500. To Thomas C.
Edwards $500. To James Edwards my brother $500. To Mary C. Edwards
dau. of Thos C. Edwards $500. To Priscilla Edwards wife of Thomas R.
Edwards, colored woman Amy & child John to Lucy Cotton. To Mary W.
Cantrell, dau. of D.H.Cantrell, negro girl. To Mary W. Cantrell dau. of
D.H.Cantrell. To L.B.Edwards. Appoint William Cantrell, D.H.Cantrell,
and L.B.Edwards exec. Pvd. February Court 1839. (P.249)

John DOBBINS - November 9, 1836 Will - To wife Nancy Dobbins land
on which I live etc. and slaves etc. To dau. Mary McMurry. To Son
Henry Dobbins 190 acres land. My four eldest sons viz. Henry, James A.,
Wm. N., and Thos C. Dobbins land said Henry Dobbins bought from his
three brothers above named, it being part of Tract I now live on. Son
William N. Dobbins hogs etc. Mentions land in western district belonging

to James /. dec'd. To son Samuel Dobbins $100, etc. To Son
Robert D. Dobbins 60 acres land. Mentions school house and
land. 'Wit: Alexander B. Dobbins, Robert Dobbins. Proved
February Court 1839. (P.250)

Joseph THOMPSON - December 24, 1836 Will - Property to
support wife and children. Appoints friend and brother-in-law
Richard Franklin, Sen'r. exec. Educate children. Wit: Jas.
L. Dyer, Edwin Marshall. Nicholas Thompson. Securities:
George T. Brown, etc. Pvd. February Court 1839. (P.251)

Kinchen LAIR - October 26, 1838 Will - Brother John Lair
1.00. Brother Bennett Lair $1.00. Sister Ducella Manning
$1.00. Sister Polly Percile $1.00. Friend Hugh D. McWhirter,
exec. 'Wit: 'Miles A. Bush, John Mulkey. Pvd. January 1839.
(P.251)

Nancy ROGAN - November 28, 1838 Will - Grandson Hugh
Logan, negro boy. Granddaughter Clarissa Rogan, negro girl.
Grandson William Rogan, negro girl. To Son Francis Rogan and
heirs, negro boy. To Son Ramond Rogan, etc. Appoint son
Francis Rogan executor. Wit: James Barr, Samuel Barr. Pvd.
March 1839. (P.252)

Lervy PRIZENDINE - February 8, 1839 Will - Wife Lucy all
estate. Daughter Sally Laine residing in Franklin County,
Virginia. Note on John Pardue of County of Franklin. Note on
Andrew Brooks of County of Franklin. To Sally Kane and her
heirs. To two sons John B. Prizindine and Richard C. Prizendine
land on where Edward Williams now lives and where Rowland F.
Hodges of Common School land. Divide between John Bard, Richard
C., etc. To daughters Rebecca Robinson and Nancy Brooke $100
each. To two sons Young Paul Prizindine and James W. Prizindine
land. To two daughters Permelia Brizindine and Polly Cochran
$100. Appoint John B. Prizindine, Richard C. Prizendine, Young P.
Prizindine, and James W. Brizindine executors. Mentions Richard
C. Prizendine, Rebecca Robertson, Nancy Brooks. Permelia
Prizendine, Polly Cochran. 'Wit: Meridith Hodge, William
Woodall. April Court 1839 Will. (P.252)

Elizabeth TAYLOR - October 31, 1838 Will - 10 acres of
land purchased of James Wallace, Esq. Land in Campbell Co,
Va., etc. My 3 daus: Polly Taylor, Jane Taylor and Elizabeth
Taylor. My other children (not by name). Appt. these 3 named
daus. exec. Wit: James Dobbin, Vernalia Curry. Pvd. May Term
1839. (P.253)

Charles LUCAS - December 20, 1838 Will - Wife Martha Lucas
land whereon I live and etc. Wife and children - my three
youngest children remain with their mother to be educated. My
children: Mary Ann Lucas, William Harrison Lucas, Hester Ann
Lucas, John Anderson Lucas, Matilda Lucas. Appoint William
Walton exec. Wit: James Douglass, J.H.House. Pvd. June 1839.
(P.253)

Joseph McCLOTHLIN - July 3, 1837 Will - To wife Polly 100 acres.
My children that is in this country all my slaves etc. My children
that maybe absent in some foreign country. Son Andrew. Sons and
daus. Joseph McGlothlin, Jr., John McGlothlin, Wm. McGlothlin, Andrew
McGlothlin, James McGlothlin, Alexander McGlothlin, Elizabeth Goostree.
Sons Joseph and William executors. Wit: James H. House, John M.
House. Securities: John C. Beard, John Graves. Pvd. June 1839. (P.255)

Joseph CARTER - September 7, 1838 Will - Wife Ann, land whereon I
now live and land purchased of Pleasant Bell 249 acres and negroes. To
my grandchildren the children of my daughter Mary Hanna $800. To my
daughter Elizabeth Simpson what I have given and certain negro slaves.
To son Joseph W. Carter what already given and etc. Land adjoining
Bledsoe. To son William Carter what already given and etc. To my dau.
Nancy Carter $50. To my three granddaughters, children of my son
Francis Carter, namely, Mary Carter, Sarah Carter, and Martha Carter,
tract land between where I live and Thomas Taylor's land, called "the
Wilson", containing 60 acres. To grandson Nathan Carter $120. Support
my wife and family. My three children: Elizabeth Simpson, Joseph W.
Carter, William M. Carter. Also Nancy Carter. Wife Ann. A division
among my own children land at my wife's death. Daughter Mary Carter.
Appoint sons Joseph W. Carter and William M. Carter exec. Wit: Thos
Gilman, Thos White. Securities: Nelson B. Turner, James H. Turner.
Pvd. July 1839. (P.256)

Isham HODGES Sr. - December 23, 1829 Will - Wife Betsy, life time
estate in all real estate and personal property. To lawful heirs of my
eldest son Asa Hodges $1.00 equally divided. To son Rowland T. Hodges
$1.00. To lawful heirs of my son Isham Hodges $1.00. To my son
Meredith Hodges $1.00. To my son William Hodges $1.00. To my son
Ezekiel C. Hodges 1 acre of land in Kentucky on side of 45 acres tract
on which he now lives on. To my dau. Patsy Ausbrooke $50.00 at decease
of my wife Betsy. Daughter Milly Hodges. Daughter Phebe Hodges, land.
My 2 grandsons, Isham H. West and David H. West. Appoint Ezekiel C.
Hodges and Meredith Hodges executors. Wit: J.B.Brizindine, William
Manod (?). Sec: J.B.Brizendine, Wm. H. Ausbrook. Proved Aug.1829
(P.258)

Mary CARNEY - September 1839 Will - My expenses be paid. To Son
David J. Carney. To dau. Elizabeth B. Carney. To dau. Mary S. Carney.
To dau. Agnes C. Carney. To dau. Priscilla Carney. Appoint Shelton
Carney exec. Wit: David Calloway, Edmond Lewis, John B. Dickerson.
October Court 1839. (P.259)

John MADDOX - September 13, 1839 Will - Wife Mary - estate keep
together, raise and school children her life. Land mentioned. Appoint
wife Mary and James Butler exec. Wit: Joseph Smith, J.B.Brizindine,
Mathew Perdue, Eli Perdue. October Court 1839. (P.260)

Ashley STANFIELD - August 27, 1839 Will - Sell land at public
auction by executors. Mentions negroes be sold, some emancipated. To
my mother-in-law Elizabeth Russell $1000 to be paid. To son Ashley
Stanfield when 21 yrs old. My relation James A. Vaughn to govern son.
Son Ashley be educated in law. Friends Henry B. Vaughn, James H. Vaughn,
Joseph Robb be exec. Test: J.A.Blackmore, W.H.Edwards. Pvd. Nov.
1839. (P.260)

James HORSLEY - June 15, 1824 Will - Have christian burial.
Wife Jane and she give our children the best she can. At wife's
death equally divide among children viz. James R. Horsley,
Louisv E. Horsley, William W. Horsley, John W. Horsley, Robert
G. Horsley, Susan J. Horsley, Eliza F. Horsley. Wife Jane and
son James R. to exec. Wit: Tolbert Horsley, Elijah Rutledge,
Charles Newman. Pvd. Nov. 1839. (P.261)

Rowland T. HODGES - October 28, 1839 Will - To son Lawson
H. Hodges. To son Ezekiel M. Hodges. To daughter Louisa
Elizabeth Hodges. To daughter Sarah Hodges. To daughter Chloe
Hodges. Wife Nancy. Owned land. Calls for John B. Hodges.
Calls for Lennon H. Hodges. Calls for Ezekiel N. Hodges. Calls
for Louisa Elizabeth Hodges. Calls for Sarah Hodges. Calls for
Chloe Hodges. Calls for Isham Hodges. Calls for Asa H. Hodges.
Wit: N. Hodges, William W. Ausbrooks. Appoints Meredith
Hodges exec. December 1839. (P.262)

Dolly LOVING wife of Walton Loving dec'd. - November 27,
1839 Will - Names sons Henry H. and John P. Loving all claim to
land I live on. To daughter Evaline bed etc. To Sarah Loving,
Henry Loving, Evaline Loving, John P. Loving, equal shares.
Wants Henry Loving to keep "my little son John P. Loving" with
him. Appoints son Henry Loving exec. Wit: John O. Higgerson,
Nicholas Stone. Securty, Alexander William. Pvd. December
1839. (P.262)

Will of Fanny ARBUTHERT - Daughter Nancy and to her
children. Daughter Rededy house and plant. My deceased daughter Cynthey and Elizabeth children. To heirs of my son
Jordon. To heirs of my son Marcus. Set my hand Nov. 4, 1839.
Proved 1839 December. (P.263)

George W. HARRISON will - My sisters son George Corn.
All property in possession of A.G.Doncho and his heirs.
October 22, 1839. Proved December 1839. (P.264)

Will of Elizabeth PERRY - To Sarah Francis $300. To Mary
Jenkins china and glass. To Susan Jane silver. Appoints
John W. Garrett to have in hand property to Sarah Francis.
Appoints Robert Patton executor. October 23, 1839. Proved
December 1839. (P.264)

Moocky JONES will to my son Gabriel. Gabriel Jones
land 25 acres. Rest my children and my husband. My youngest
son Peter Jones. April 25, 1839. Proved 1839 Oct. (P.265)

Will of Robert WHITE, wife Lucretia. July 27, 1839.
Proved October 1839. (P.265)

Francis WHITE will. To Amanda Malvina Dickerson. To
Augulina Dickerson. To Louisa M. Corndiner. My brothers and
friend Charles H. White Sr. Exec. January 2, 1830. Proved
February 1840. (P.265)

70

Thomas TAYLOR will - Wife Milly Taylor. Children John Taylor, Polly Taylor, James Taylor, Elizabeth FLOWERS, Annie Taylor, Pleasant Taylor, Jonathan Taylor, David Taylor, Wm. Taylor. Appoints son William Taylor executor. April 10, 1836. Proved February 1836. (P.267)

Will of Judy WEATHERFORD - Sister Weatherford named Nancy land in Tenn. and Ky. and Virginia. Her five children Mary Ann Weatherford, Edline Weatherford, Ednes Weatherford, Emily B. Weatherford, Hilary E. Weatherford. Appoints Samuel Davis executor. July 23, 1839. Proved 1840. (P.267)

Will of Robert A. KING - Aunt Elizabeth King. Wife Nancy J. Educate children. 7 children not all of age. My father Richard King deceased. Appoints J.W.Baldridge executor. March 25, 1840. William McCall was one of witnesses. (P.267)

Will of G. W. HARRISON - Sisters son George Carr. A.G.Donoho executor. October 21, 1839. Proved July 1840. (P.269)

Martha S. HARRIS will - Neice Francis Muievna Robinson. Appoints M.L.Sharp (M.L.F.Sharpe), Executor. June 20, 1840. Proved Aug 1840. (P.269)

Will of Susanna HANNA - Son James H. Hanna. Son Abner L. Hanna. Daughter Katherine Hanna. Three children James B., Abner L. and Katherine. James Hanna dead mentioned. Son James P. Hanna executor. July 24, 1838. Proved August 1840. (P.270)

Isaac WALTON will - Son John B. Wife Elizabeth. Daughter Kitty Barker. Son John B. Tract land I purchased from Wm. Burs except 2 acres where the Meating House stands I reserve for use of people of the neighborhood. Daughter Polly Hogan. Daughter Carolina Luton. Children son Jeriah, Elizabeth, Tennie, Nancy Connell, Sally Harris, Caroline LOOTON, William Walton and Ollive Connal. November 1, 1838. (P.270) (See full copy)

Michael SHANNON will - Land in Robertson County, Son Harvey Shannon. September 25, 1840. (P.271)

Zachariah GREEN will - August 13, 1838 - Daughter Elizabeth Hudson. Daughter Peggy Hardin. Grandson Jackson Moore. Daughter Emily Teasdel. (P.272)

John DICKSON will - Wife Elizabeth and children. Three children James B., Reuben D. and Lucy S. August 31, 1840. (P.272)

Malinda TURNER will - December 21, 1840. Proved January 1841. Brother John H. Turner. Interest in my father's estate John Turner. Niece Mary Ann Turner daughter of my brother John. Niece Louisa Eliza Turner infant dau. of my brother John. Sister Sarah Turner wife of my brother John. My brother John C. Turner. (P.273)

John BOYD will - Wife Mary. Son Cyrus 160 acres I live on. Children Elizabeth Allen. Robert Boyd. Ann Chandler. Sarak Duke. Cyrus Boyd. October 18, 1836. Proved 1841. (P.274)

71

Isaac WALTON will - Son John B. Wife Elizabeth. Daughter
Kitty Barker. Mentions land from Lucy A. Baker. Land I purchased
from Wm. Bur across from Meeting House to be reserved for people
of the neighborhood etc. Daughter Kiddy Baker. Daughter Polly
Hogan land on waters Madison Creek. Mentions Isaac W. Moore.
Daughter Caroline Luton land. Son Jeriah H. Walton. Elizabeth
Tennie, Nancy Connell. Sally Harris, Caroline Looton, Wm.
Walton, Olive Connal. Appoints three sons Josiah, William and
John B. Walton exec. November 1, 1838. Codicil my children.
Polly Hogan, Josiah Walton, Elizabeth Tennis, Nancy Connell,
Sally Harris, William Walton, Caroline Sutton, Kiddy Baker, Oliver
Connel. March 21, 1839. Proved September 1840. (P.270)

Michael SHANNON will - My companion Margaret Shannon.
Land sold to William Mose of Robertson Co. Son Harvey Shannon.
September 25, 1840. Proved October 1840. Witnessed by Wm. A.
Whitworth, Joseph Coffman. (P.271)

Zachariah GREEN will - Daughter Elizabeth Hudson. Dau-
ghter Peggy Harden. Grandson Jackson Moore. Granddaughter
Emily Tesdel. Grandson Zachariah Hudson. Land I bought of
Isaac Turner. Two friends Frederick Watkins and Doctor John
Franklin executors. August 12, 1838. Proved October 1840.
(P.272)

John DICKERSON will - Wife Elizabeth. Three children
John P., Reuben D. and Lucy S. August 31, 1840. Proved
October 1840. (P.272)

Elizabeth MANSKER will - Emancipate negro slaves. My
neighbor Charles L. Boyd to take charge of negroes and remove
them either to the State of Indiana, Illinois, or Ohio and
leave them free. Charles B. Pyron to receive for his services
performed $150. Leaves negroes various sums of money. Appoints
Isaac Walton Esqr. and Charles L. Byron exec. September 20,
1825. No children mentioned. Proved May 1841. (P.277)

John McMURTRY will - Wife Peggy plantation on which I
live. My sister Jane Hammons house and lot where John Carrott
Jr. now lives. Children: Henry, John, Asa, Thomas, Wilkerson
McMurtry, James Garrett, Polly Forester. Executors Asa McMurtry,
Thomas Wilkerson McMurtry, and Samuel Kirkpatrick. September
6, 1831. Proved April Court 1841. (P.278)

1840. John ASKLEY will - Wife have plantation I live on.
Two sons John W. and Leonard Askey. To Howard Lewis and his
heirs place he now lives. Daughter Nancy. Son Elisha. Proved
July 1841. (P.279)

Henry McADEN will - Wife Mary all property. Son Hugh land
I live on at wife's death. Three daughters Judy Neely. Kather-
ine S. Bradley, Mary H. Meadow. Appoints David Carney and Joseph
G. Meadow executors. April 3, 1841. Proved August 1841. (P.279)

Robert HAWKINS will - Wife Sarah F. Daughter Frances Hunt.
Children and grandchildren James K. Hawkins one ninth part. Eliza S.
Jones one ninth part. Two granddaughters children of my dau. Amey D.
Webb deceased. One ninth to Wm. Hawkins. One ninth to Charles G.(T.?)
Hawkins. One ninth to Joseph G. Hawkins. One ninth to Sarah H. Hawkins.
One ninth to Rachel G. Hawkins. One ninth to Stephen R. Gulliam Hawkins.
January 17, 1840. Proved March 1840. (P.274)

Josiah A. ALEXANDER will - Land I bought from James Starck to be
sold. Land I bought from Henry Head be sold. Wife Susannah one third.
Son James L. Daughter Francis Eliza. Son James L. Appoints wife and
John J. Hibbett exec. January 31, 1840 Proved March 1840. (P.275)

Noncupative will of Jane HENDERSON.- John Carney Jr. and John
Carney S. asked to be witnesses on her death bed. Son Samuel K.
Henderson. March 1, 1841. (P.276)

Susannah ALEXANDER will - Land I live on 40 acres. Head and foot
stone to husband M. Alexander, and my grave, and enclose in stone wall.
Two children Francis Eliza and James L. Alexander. Exec. John J.
Hibbett. December 12, 1840. Proved March 1849. (P.276)

Shelton CARNEY will - Wife Susan tract land I live on during life
of Mrs. Frances Charlton. My children: Fanny L., Mary A., Susan E.,
David G., Elizabeth K., Joshua, Manerva A., John S., Dan P. Carney.
May 24, 1841. Proved September 1841. (P.280)

John GROOMS will - Wife Elizabeth household goods, etc. Son-in-law
Samuel Johnson. Cash in hands of William Sadler. March 3, 1840. Proved
November 1841. (P.280)

George READON will - Son William one half land I live on. Wife
Elizabeth Readon. Son Richard H. Readon. Two daughters Martha Readon
and Mary G. Young. Four children. Appoints son Richard H. Readon and
James S. Douglass, executors. October 22, 1841. Proved October 22,
1841. December court 1841. (P.281)

Thomas STONE will - Wife Matilda M. Stone one third tract land
house and spring lying on Cumberland River. My children oldest Granville
Stone. My daughter Fanny Hrower. Son Thomas Stone. Children Sidney,
Jules, Samuel Stone, Moranda Shaver, Maranda Shaver, James Stone. Robert
Stone, Matilda Stone, James Stone, Granville Stone, Fanny Thrower,
Thomas Stone, Sidney Jiles, Matilda Stone. Mentions Frances Youree.
Codicil July 15, 1841 mentions brother Edmiston's estate. Appoints son
Samuel and Jacob Cook executors. September 9, 1840. Proved September
9, 1840. (P.282)

Mead MAY will - To Mary May. Appoints James S. Douglass executor.
February 3, 1841. Proved February 3, 1841. (P.283)

Benjamine COFFMAN will - September 18, 1841 - Sister Julia Jane
Cuffman. Appoints Joseph Cuffman and Edward Spurrur exec. Proved
January 1842. (P.284)

73

John B. HOWARD wish Charles Grimm to administer over my
estate. My wife and children. Wife Margaret. Proved February
1842. (P.285)

Samuel COCHRAN Sr. will - Wife Sarah Cochran. My daughter
Nancy. My late daughter Jermima Hodges now dead. Daughter
Sarah Hodges. Son William B. Cochran. Daughter Polly Mattox.
Daughter Elizabeth Prizendone. Son Samuel. Son-in-law John P.
Prizendine. March 8, 1835. Codicil. Proved February 1842.
(P.285)

Elizabeth LAMPATH will - October 3, 1841 - Son James W.
Daughter Polly Clouge. Mentions guardian of James W. Proved
February 1842. (P.286)

Jesse SKEEN will - Daughter Nancy McGlothlin wife of William
negroes and my old Mill tract in Simpson Co, Ky. Daughter Sarah
Groves wife of John Groves $1.00. Daughter Elizabeth Skein all
land which I purchased on east side Drakes Creek. Son Kinion
Taylor Skeen land. Daughter Caroline Butler wife of John Butler.
My daughter Rachel Meador wife of Anderson A. Meador. My son
Alexander David Skeen. My daughter Charity Skeen land on
Drakes Creek. Mentions land adjoining Huanoah Taylor tract.
Mentions land adjoining Spoute Spring south to Rachel Caldwell.
Mentions land adjoining Gribler. Mentions land adjoining
Charles W. Williams. Mentions land adjoining Benjamine Mabery.
Son John G. Skeen my McKinney tract of land. Daughter Polly
Skeen tract land west of my daughter Charitys. Mentions Black-
smith Shop due South of Baskerville line. Three dumb daughters
Elizabeth, Charity, and Polly. Benjamin Mabrey tract land be
sold. Executors Jinison T. Skeen and John G. Skeen. March 24,
1840. December 24, 1841. Proved March 1842. (P.287)

Thomas DONNELLS will - Son Levy. Three grandsons John
Hassell Donnell, Thomas Whitfield Donnell, William Donnell. My
granddaughter Eliza Bain. To the Presbyterian General Associa-
tion Board of Missions of education $100. Grandchildren Robert
W. Donnell. Son Levy. Grandchildren John Hassell Donnell,
Grandson Thomas Whitefield Donnell. Grandson William Donnell.
Granddaughter Harriet W. Bain. Granddaughter Sophia Bain. I
give Scots family bible to my three grandsons J.H., T.W., and
Wm. Donnell. Other books divided among them and Rober Washington
Donnell. Son Levy and John Wallace executors. December 4, 1845.
Codicil. Grandchildren not all of age. December 4, 1835.
Proved March 1842. (P.289)

Grant SUTE will - Wife Lily Sute, my farm I live on.
Daughter Sally Ross. Vickery Frazier. My grandson John Sute,
Two grandchildren Nancy and James Huston, Grandson John Sute.
Appoints James P. Taylor executor. March 23, 1840. Proved
March 1842. (P.290)

Edward WILLIAMS will - My grandchildren Louis Stephen
Mitchell. Hugh Mitchell. Edmond Mitchell. Amelia Williams
(alias Gucher). Margaret Watwood. Alexander Watwood. Isaac B.

74

Williams. Buron Williams. Grandson Josephus Williams. Divide certain property between Stephen Mitchell, Hugh Mitchell, Edward Mitchell, Margaret Watwood, Alexander Watwood, Marian Williams, Amelia Tucker, Isaac B. Williams. To Ismiah Preston Gilbert $100.00. To James T. Gilbert. My son Jno Williams. To Julia B. Briggs $1.00. My daughter-in-law Jane Williams. My grandson Benjamine F. Williams. Appoints Abram Bradley and Meredith Hodges executors. February 21, 1839. Proved April 1842. (P.289)

William DAVENPORT will - Children to receive education. Wife Four children Mary, John, James, Tom equally divided. Appoints Thomas Bryson and Presley Bradford executors. July 13, 1832. Proved April 1842. (P.291)

Jacob C. COOK will - Children Mary Catherine not of age 16. Adline Eliza. Marcus Lafayette Cook. Two twin boys James and Henry not of age. Wife Matilda. Appoints Elisha Poddie and Robert Desha executors. Henry Cook of Huntsville, Executor. June 27, 1825. Proved April 1842. (P.292)

Jesse HAYNIE will - Son Elijah. Daughter Elizabeth White. Son George. Son Jesse. Son Louis. Granddaughter formerly Mary Haynie now Mary Downey. Granddaughter Francis Davison daughter of Judah Davinson. Daughter Harriet C. Haynie. My daughter Caroline Moore. Wife Francis A. Haynie. Two daughters Caroline H. Hall and Harriett C. Haynie. Appoints Louis Haynie and Wm. Hall exec. March 3, 1842. Proved May 1842. (P.293)

William WILLIAMS will - Wife Elizabeth C. land I live on. Son Francis Williams. Son Zachariah Williams. Children of Zachariah Williams. Son Alexander Williams. Daughter Patsy Martin Cox. Son Wm. B. Williams. Young son Joseph C.G.Williams. Grandchildren left by my dec'd daughter Polly I. Mabry. Children of deceased son John B. Williams. Friends Joseph Robb and Joel Parish exec. March 16, 1842. Proved May 1842. (P.293)

Archibale SKIPPENITH will - Wife Elizabeth property. Two sons Austin P. and Wm. S. exec. November 22, 1841. Proved May 1842. (P.294).

Ezekiel MARSHALL will - To heirs of my daughter Jimsay Caps not dec'd. Viz, Dock Rosannah and Ansulet and Elizabeth Caps, now living with me. Daughter Elizabeth Gaines. Daughter Anna Brooks. Daughter Francis Durham. Son Eli Marshall tract land I live on. Wife Lucy. Son Eli exec. Son-in-law Wm. Burham, exec. May 16, 1836. Proved June 1842. (P.295)

David ALSUP will - Wife Martha all. Five children Rahal Eshley. Jeremiah Alsup, Edna Tracy. Sally Woods. Martha Hiden. Appoints friend Moses H. Herring executor. March 23, 1842. Proved June 1842. (P.295)

CORRECTIONS

Page 10: For William <u>Brown</u> read <u>Bowen</u> (May 6, 1804).

Page 13 (John Trice will): For <u>Keefe</u> read <u>Keezee</u>.

Page 33 (Richard Wilks will): For <u>Anna</u> Wynne read <u>Martha Ann.</u>

Page 40, 8th line from top: For <u>Lane</u> Smith read <u>Larrie</u>.

Page 43, 15th line from top: For Samuel A. <u>Brown</u> read <u>Bowen</u>.

Page 43 (James Sanders will): For wife <u>Lucerissa</u> read <u>Levise</u>;
    for William <u>Brown</u> read <u>Bowen</u>.

Page 44 (Mary H. Bowen will): For <u>Louisa</u> Sanders read <u>Levisa</u>;
    for <u>Hoebland</u> Sanders read <u>Hubbard</u>.

Page 73 (Thomas Stone will): For daughter Fanny <u>Hrower</u> read <u>Thrower</u>.

I N D E X

Note: These abstracts have been made from the original record books in the Court House, Gallatin, Sumner County, Tennessee. The script in many instances is almost impossible to translate. The spelling used herein is as near the original as may be deciphered; the spelling of many names appear incorrect to the actual spelling of the name. In several instances, the wills appear to have been recorded twice, therefore, duplications do exist. ERW

Abston 38
Acrey 63
Adams 19
Alderson 17, 50, 65
Alexander 9, 14, 19
  21, 29, 32, 34,
  37, 39, 46, 48,
  49, 52, 73
Alison 53
Allen 11, 23, 37,
  49, 59, 60, 71
Alley 63
Allison 15, 42, 53
Alsup 75
Alvis 24
Anderson 7, 9, 10,
  11, 14, 23,
  29, 32, 33, 48,
  56,
Angan 50
Anthony 20, 57
Arbuthert 70
Archer 14
Archeron 17
Armfield 64
Armstrong 8, 11, 14
Arnold 38
Asbrooks 9
Ashbrooks 9
Ashford 59
Asken 56
Askley 72
Aspley 58, 72
Atchinson 59
Atchison 59, 63
Aunley 19
Austrook 56, 69
Ausbrooke 69, 70
Austin 45
Avent 5, 21
Axum 37

Pacard 56
Badgett 23, 48
Bailey 47
Bain 39, 74
Baker 13, 17, 18, 38
  72
Baldridge 71
Ball 25, 26, 40 48, 52
Ballew 3
Bandy 34, 51
Barham 55, 59, 42
Barreird 59, 63
Barr 10, 21, 53,
  65, 67, 68
Barrett 37
Basil 53
Barnes 5, 19, 57,
  59, 63
Barron 22
Barrot 22
Barrow 7, 22, 59
Barry 14, 22, 32,
  67
Baskerville 66
Pass 44, 65
Baxter 19
Bayne 39
Baynes 52
Beakley 7
Blades 18
Bean 8
Beard 11, 20, 69.
Bearden 64, 65
Beardin 65
Bearding 65
Bearnard 17
Beasley 49
Beddy 32
Bell 12, 20. 18, 19,
  9, 40, 48, 51, 56,
  66, 69
Belote 10, 17, 35,
  41, 44, 43, 67

Bender 55
Bennett 21, 37, 57
Benthall 6, 22, 34,
Bentley 10, 16, 48,
Billany 46
Bishop 28
Black 18
Blackard 32
Blaides 18
Blackmore (Blakemore)
  1, 6, 13, 40, 47,
  44, 48, 54, 67,
  69, 60, 28
Bloodworth 9, 21
Blythe 7, 14, 25, 48
  47, 50, 53
Bledsoe 1, 2, 3, 4,
  5, 20, 27, 30, 54
  60
Blayingame 22
Bodget 47
Bloyd 5
Boddie 32, 45, 46, 47,
  59, 61, 75
Bohannan 19
Bohein 42
Boles 8
Bone 3
Booth 57
Boren 20
Bosley 1
Bottrip 38
Bowdselt 66
Bowen (Bowan) 21, 34,
  42, 43, 44, 60
Bowling 24
Boyd 71, 72
Boyers 41
Boykin 22
Boyle 50, 16
Boyles 53,
Boyls 47

Brackin 16, 33, 57

Bradford 18, 47, 53, 65, 75

Bradley 6, 21, 14, 32, 46, 39, 47, 59, 75

Bradshaw 39, 67

Brandon 11, 12, 67

Brasel 40

Brashiers 54

Bressie 54

Brien 10

Brigance 4, 7, 17, 19, 22

Briggs 75

Briley 38

Brison 27

Brinkley 59

Brizendine(Brizendone) 68, 69, 74

Brocks 75

Brocke 55, 68

Brooks 12, 68

Brown 7, 8, 10, 14, 15, 22, 25, 39, 41, 27, 62, 63, 68, 56, 27, 33, 34, 43, 66

Bruce 8, 26, 27

Bryson 34,

Bunton 10

Buckley 59

Buckner 57

Bugg 21, 51

Bullins 41

Bullus 41

Butler 69, 74

Bur 72

Burley 50

Burnet 62

Burs 71

Burton 22, 26

Busby 22, 50, 51,

Bush 8, 13, 51, 68

Bushm 2,

Buson 45

Butterworth 55

Buyans 14

Byron 72

Byrn 19

Burns 16

Byrns 27

Byzor 33, 49, 50

Byram 18

Cage 4, 6, 15, 35, 41, 44, 46, 50, 59, 64, 65

Cain 6

Calaway 54

Caldwell 60, 74

Calhoun 53, 58

Calloway 69

Camp 53

Campbell 5, 7, 11, 12, 28, 44

Cannon 67

Cantrell 42, 43, 44, 67

Capps 58

Carney 55, 69, 72, 73

Caps 75

Carothers 15, 20, 29

Carr 3, 6, 15, 52, 55, 59, 60, 71

Carrell 21

Carrol 61

Carroll 41

Carson 42

Carter 1, 4, 23, 50, 60, 69

Cartwright 5, 13, 21

Cates 29

Carthon 24

Catron 3

Catty 55

Cavatt 32

Cavin 15

Chambers 67

Chenault 45

Chandler 71

Chapman 7, 10, 53, 62

Charloss 49

Cheek 10

Christmas 2

Clabun 15

Clack 14

Clark 21, 30

Clarkson 51

Clay 5

Clemey 62

Clendening 1, 4, 30

Cline 34

Cloar 17, 30, 38

Clouge 74

Clucke 12

Coal 10

Cobb 50

Cochran 8, 68, 74

Cooke 23

Coffman 72, 73

Ccle 37

Coleman 64

Colger 17

Conn 15, 22

Connal 71, 72

Connell 57, 71, 72

Cook 11, 40, 73, 75

Cooper 15, 17, 18

Cope 10

Corn 70

Corndiner 70

Cotes 2

Cotton 4, 6, 14, 17, 19, 22, 46, 65, 67, 53, 49

Coursen 26

Cowden 16, 31

Cowen 8

Cowin 28

Cox 75

Crabb 52

Crafford 4

Corethers 18

Crain 16, 17, 23

Crane 46

Craven 18

Cravens 1, 2, 18

Crawford 6

Crenshaw 19, 22, 30, 53

Crocket 22, 28

Cromwell 3

Crunk 62

Crutcher 4

Crutchfield 5

Cruthers 4

Cryer 6, 14, 17, 40, 59

Cuffman 73

Cummings 7, 14, 65

Cummins 65

Cunningham 21

Curry 27, 61, 68

Dalton 55

Daniel 46

Dano 7

Darnal 40

Daugherty 57

Davenport 33, 75

Davis 4, 9, 25,
40, 56, 62, 67, 71
Davinson 75
Davison 75
Dawson 2, 5
Dedricks 44
Defrees 45
Deloach 3, 5
Dement 19
Denning 64, 65
Denny 40
Depuey 32
Desha 2, 3, 4, 23,
34, 59, 75
Dickeson 54
Dickerson 26, 27, 38,
37, 61, 69, 70, 72
Dickins 38
Dickson 71
Diener 44
Dillard 30
Dinning 16, 59
Dismukes 57
Dixon 10
Dobbin 68
Dobbins 20, 67, 68
Doherty 13
Donalson 3, 15
Donelson 1, 26,
Donnell 11, 15, 18,
21, 58, 59, 74
Donnells 74
Donoho 70, 71, 14,
16, 29, 30, 58
Donohoo 8
Dorris 56, 57, 64
Doss 42
Dotson 38
Douglas 1, 2, 5, 6,
9, 10, 19, 16,
61, 73, 56, 59,
11
Douglass 4, 7, 14,
16, 19, 28, 34, 35,
41, 46, 54, 55, 56,
57, 58, 61, 67
Dowell 23
Downey 74
Downs 32
Drummond 23
Duffer 52
Dugger 21, 24, 29
Duke 71
Duncan 7, 56
Dunhell 58
Dunn 2

Durham 34, 40,
56, 60, 75
Dyer 7, 22, 68

Easley 23, 48
Eshley 75
Eddins 41
Edson 64
Elmiron 24
Edmiston 73
Edwards 2, 7, 11,
14, 19, 24, 40,
42, 43, 45, 46,
53, 67, 69
Eilks 60
Ekols 37
Eliston 49
Elliston 59
Ellace 25, 26, 27
Elliott 7, 8, 25,
26, 49, 61
Ellis 10, 25, 29,

Elliss 27
Evans 5, 65
Erwin 33
Espey 27
Estis 25
Ewing 49, 50
Exam 10
Exum 15

Far 9
Fearn 34
Featherston 18, 21
Feelwood 55

Ferguson 54
Fenner 8
Ferrel 16, 20
Ferrin 8
Field 59
Fielks 56
Figures 53, 58
Fulghum 20
Findley 14
Finley 22, 40
Fisher 45
Fitzhugh 24
Fleming 23
Fletcher 19
57
Flippin 37
Flowers 71
Fonville 44
Ford 64

Forester 72
Foster 33, 67
Foxall 59
Francis 70
Frady 45
Franklin 3, 47, 6,
64, 65, 55, 72,
57, 68
Frazier 74
Frazor 2
Freedle 53
Fuller 54
Fulton 28
Furgerson 38

Gaines 57, 75
Galbreath 9, 1
Gambling 58
Gardner 9, 12, 21,
47, 48
Garrett 10, 42, 72
Garrott 72
George 2, 16
Gibson 7, 10, 27
Gifte 38
Gilbert 75
Giles 7, 9, 13, 21
Gill 15
Gillam 20
Gillespie 12, 20,
24, 27, 50,
18
Gilliham 10
Gilliam 32, 33, 52,
57
Gilman 69
Gilmer 9
Glasgow 46
Glass 5
Glen 13
Glover 21, 22, 41,
51
Gohen 12
Goodale 42
Goodman 20
Goostree 69
Gordon 19
Goudy 7
Gowdy 9
Grace 10
Graham 18, 19, 27
Grainger 14, 19, 24
Granger 9, 67
Graves (Groves) 19,
59, 69, 74, 64
Gray 49, 50, 66

Grear 45.
Green (Greene) 1, 20, 38, 39, 47, 54, 55, 56, 71, 72
Greer 10
Greensley 28
Gregory 47, 29, 33, 45
Gribler 74
Grier 15
Griffith 62
Grigg 5
Grimm 46, 74
Grimsley 16, 49
Grooms 40, 73
Guthrey 53
Guthrie 67
Gwin 8, 9, 14, 22, 1
Gwinn 9, 37, 43

Hacker 3
Hadley 1
Haffengton 24
Hail 23, 66
Hale 15, 35, 37, 47
Hall 2, 12, 20, 24, 23, 52, 53, 54, 58, 67, 75, 32, 50
Hamelton 21, 29, 22
Hambleton 16
Hamilton 3, 5, 7, 14, 29, 33, 34, 54
Hamlet 65
Hamlin 63
Hammond 38, 64
Hammons 72, 2
Hampton 5
Handley 43
Hanna 19, 55, 58, 67, 71, 69
Hannah 3, 1
Hanner 19, 14
Harden 19, 72
Hardin 11, 71
Hardy 26, 40, 65
Hareford 8
Hargraves (Hargroves) 66
Hargrove 21, 66
Harker 3
Harney 3, 51

Harper 49, 50, 51, 62
Harpole 6
Harrington 5
Harris 12, 13, 17, 20, 21, 19, 28, 31, 32, 50, 59, 71, 72
Harrison 52, 67, 70, 71
Hart 2, 10, 14, 21, 29, 34, 45, 54.
Harten 23, 60
Harvey 50
Hassell 11, 13, 14, 43, 59, 67, 45
Hasten 23, 10
Haudyshall 29
Haues 37
Haw 17
Hawkins 7, 73
Haynes 52, 67
Haynie 42, 43, 75
Head 17, 27, 73
Headon 10
Heart 42
Helbays 22
Hellen 6
Henderson 12, 25, 30, 34, 73
Hendon 52
Hendrick 12
Hendricks 3, 63
Henley 60
Henold 31
Henry 6, 9, 22, 33, 40, 48, 56
Herman 29
Herring 75
Hethly 8
Hibbett 73
Hicks 10, 24
Hiden 75
Higgerson 70
Higison 29
Hill 59
Hillay 62
Hillays 22
Hinson 24
Hobday 6, 57, 65, 63
Hodge 25, 37, 51, 69, 70
Hodges 42, 66, 67, 68, 69, 70, 75, 56, 74, 63

Hogan 14, 71, 72
Hogin 3, 7
Holland 12
Hollis 8, 18, 58
Hollisson 21
Holloway 19
Holly 50
Holmes 8, 13, 66
Horton 41
Horsley 70
Horsly 27, 70
Hoskins 8
Hosley 65
Hotihkiss 17
Hougham 56
House 12, 37, 47, 48, 59, 69, 68
Howard 15, 19, 20, 39, 56, 65, 74
Howdestilt 66
Howell 6, 47, 19, 52
Hrower 73
Hubbert 8, 38
Hubert 17, 38, 61
Hudson 16, 29, 51, 64, 71, 72
Huffington 24
Hughes 4
Humphrey 20
Humphreys 23, 24
Hunt 15, 16, 28, 21, 23, 49, 52, 73
Hunter 24, 38, 51, 59, 64
Huston 74
Hutcherson 65, 66
Hutchins 16, 25
Hutchinson 3
Hutson 64
Hyman 2

Inman 45
Irby 55
Isbell 15
Isley 55
Irwin 9

Jackson 2, 16, 32, 64
James 63
Jefferson 39
Jenkins 70

Jennings 53
Jessee 62
Jiles 73
Johnson 11, 13, 21,
  15, 23, 40, 62,
  67, 73
Johnston 5, 60
Joiner 8
Jones 2, 3, 1, 16,
  18, 40, 41, 27,
  52, 56, 58, 64,
  70, 73
Jorden (Jordan) 12
Jouthrie (Guthrie)
  67
Joyner (Joiner) 38,
  43
Justice 66
Justin 66

Kane 68
Kealey 7
Keber 67
Keefe 13, 57, 61
Keen 8, 33
Keese 40, 48
Kelough 21
Kennedy 14, 37
Kenney 1
Kerr 10, 23, 51
Ketring 29
Key 18, 31, 56
Killgore 23
Kindrick 5
King 11, 13, 14, 7
  17, 18, 48, 53,
  58, 62, 71, 43
Kirk 16, 53
Kirkham 63, 66
Kirkpatrick 24, 40,
  45, 46, 48, 63,
  72
Kittrell 65
Kitring 29, 48
Kizer 64
Knox 11

Lacey 34
Lackey 34
Laine 68
Lair 68
Lambath 16, 46, 74
Lane 15, 23, 53
Lanier 66
Lanner 3
Larenn 7

Larrence (Lawrence,
  Laurence) 12, 16,
  57
Lassiter (Laseter,
  Lasater) 22, 23,
  24, 63
Latimer (Latimore) 8,
  12, 16, 43, 52,
  62
Lauderson 64
Lauderdale 5, 6, 7,
  34, 42, 66
Lawson 52
Layne 18
Layon 67
Leabey (Seabry) 6
Leath 22
Lemmons 24
Lester 64
Lewis 55, 69, 72
Lindsay (Lindsey) 8,
  16, 17
Linkey 49
Linsey 10
Little 34, 38
Locke 16
Logan 19
Long 39, 47
Looney 1, 5, 8,
  4, 43, 45, 61
Love 15
Lovel (Lovell) 50,
  65
Loving 70
Lowery 40
Lucas 68
Lum 3
Lunn 4
Luton (Looton, Luthin)
  1, 38, 64, 71,
  72
Lyning 48
Lyon 40
Lyons 53

McAdams 13
McAdon (McAdin) 15,
  72
McBee 3
McCadam 7
McCafferty 10, 11,
  33, 71
McCarty 15
McCauliston 3
McCallister
  (McCollister) 4,
  16

McClenahan 7
McColough 55
McConnell 17
McCorkle 11, 17
McCowden 31
McDaniel 30
McGlothlin
  (McLothlin) 52,
  62, 63, 65, 74
McGuire 12, 34,
  42
McKain 1, 4
McKelworth 2
McKendree 20, 50,
  59
McKissack 31, 52
McKitchen 43
McKnight 40, 48
McKoin 57
McLeurath 39
McManney 9
McMillen 5
McMurry 31
McMurtry 38, 72
McNiell 43
McNutt 14
McWhirter 2, 68

Maacey 16
Mabery (Maberry)
  (Mabry) 63, 74,
  75
Maddox 69
Maglohom 8
Mahan 34
Maines 17
Malone 67
Maloon 5
Man 9
Manning 67, 68
Manod 69
Mansker 2, 31, 72
Marlin 8, 39
Marlon 17
Marshall 9, 62, 67,
  68, 75
Martin 1, 6, 15, 22,
  18, 34, 46, 50,
  67, 28, 59
Masten (Mastin) 1, 26
Mattox 74
May (Mays) 19, 62, 63,
  65, 73
Meador 30, 74
Meadow 51, 72
Melton 20, 56

Mercer 18, 51
Merry 51
Meston 26
Miers 40
Miller 31
Mills 6, 29, 47
Milner 12
Milton 15
Minor 38
Mitchell 12, 16,
 13, 22, 29, 49,
 54, 56, 45, 67,
 74
Montgomery 7, 28,
 66, 46, 56
Moodrill 9
Moor 17
Moore 9, 10, 23,
 28, 29, 38, 41,
 43, 44, 54, 67,
 71, 72, 75
Moorehead 7, 47
More 9, 52

Morgan 38, 64
Morrison 11
Morton 17
Mose 72
Moss 11
Motheral (Motherall)
 10, 15, 18, 21,
Mountflorence 8
Mucklerath 53
Mulkey 68
Murfree 45
Murper 15
Murrey 9, 23
Murrings 10
Murry 1, 58
Myers 50

Nafe 62
Neale 28
Neely 4, 2, 26,
 27, 72
Newberry 57
Newman 70
Newton 3
Neilson 13, 66
Nolan 65
Norman 11
Norris 12, 28, 21
Nusom 5
Nuckles 57
Nye 10, 13, 14,
 30
Nicholls 4

Odom (Odum) 4, 49,
 59, 67
Orgain 21
Oglesby 10?
Oldham 2, 64
Ore (Orr) 12, 13,
 39, 41
Ormane (Ormond)
 29, 62
Overby 20
Owen 19, 50
Ozbrook 14

Palmer 47
Pardue 68
Parker 2, 10, 16,
 17, 39, 42, 57,
 60, 62, 65
Parkerson 10
Parnal 20
Parr 16
Parrish (Parish)
 51, 53, 64, 65,
 75
Patterson 33, 45,
 52, 59
Patton 13, 20, 29,
 33, 45, 46, 63,
 70
Payne 52, 63
Pearce (Pearse)
 (Pierce) 31, 49,
 51, 54
Pearcy 17
Peck 50
Peek 20
Peel 4
Peny 2
Penny 4, 6, 14
Percile 68
Perdue 54, 69
Perkins 67
Perry 2, 13, 34,
 38, 70
Pettus 12
Peyton 4, 57, 67
Phagan 67
Pherry 66
Phillips 2, 7,
 11, 18, 35
Phipps 15
Pigg 23
Pittman 21, 41
Pitts 17, 18, 58
Parkerson 10
Pleasant 47
Park 4

Polk 9, 17, 29,
 31, 54
Porter 17
Potts 54
Powell 13
Prescott 57
Preston 21, 25,
 27
Preivitt 21
Price 24
Proctor 65
Provine 1
Pruthet 10
Pryor 3
Puckett 39
Pugh 8
Pullen 3
Purvis 23, 47

Quarles 25

Ragsdale 54
Randy 8
Rankin 47
Rawlings 7, 19,
 39, 56, 66
Ray 66
Read 15, 21,
 49, 50, 65
Readon 73
Redditt 37
Reed 5, 15, 17,
 40, 49, 54
Reese 23
Reid 42
Rhodes 28
Rice 4, 11
Richardson 16, 64
Richmond 49
Rickman 22, 23,
 33, 50, 56
Roan 48
Robb 11, 21, 29,
 50, 51, 67, 69
Roe 15
Robert 18
Roberts 5, 20, 22,
 40
Robertson 24, 25,
 37, 52, 53, 66,
 68
Robinson 3, 4, 9,
 12, 15, 68, 71
Rogan 1, 2, 5,
 17, 68
Rogers 6, 8, 13,
 31, 39

Roney 10, 16, 19,
  22, 59
Roper 10
Ross 74
Routon 47
Rowland 32
Rowlings 49
Ruff 24
Rule (Ryle) 1, 2,
  18, 55
Ruse 8
Russell ..., 44, 69
Rutherford 11, 12,
  65
Rutledge 16, 70
Ruuse 13

Sadler 3, 73
Sand 40
Sanders (Saunders) 2,
  5, 12, 21, 25,
  26, 27, 28, 29,
  31, 40, 43, 44,
  45, 47, 48, 49,
  50, 51, 54
Sanford 42
Savaly 64
Scobey 61
Scean 17
Scot 20
Scott 4, 20, 29,
  67
Scruggs 57
Scurlock 61, 60
Searcy 2, 57
Sears 59
Seawell 7, 9, 22,
  38, 49, 55
Seay 60
Sellers 34
Senter 58
Shannon 71, 72
Sharp 1, 11, 18,
  67, 71
Shavor 40
Shavin 3, 4
Shaw 52
Shearon 48
Shelby 1, 4, 7,
  17, 20, 22, 23,
  30, 34
Shelton 18, 37,
  67
Sheperd 53
Shippen 14
Short 39
Shote 37

Shoulders 54, 63
Shy (Sly) 53
Simpkins 15
Simmons 7, 20
Simpson 9, 12, 31,
  57, 66, 69
Sims 21
Singleton 21
Skeen (Skein) 74
Skippeneth 75
Sloan 7, 9, 11,
  15, 21, 25,
  26, 30
Sloss 18, 21
Smart 32
Smothers 15, 19
Smith 4, 9, 13,
  15, 17, 18, 20,
  21, 25, 26, 31,
  35, 40, 44, 45,
  48, 51, 57, 60,
  61, 62, 65, 66,
  69
Smoddy 7, 17, 37
Southall 67
Soula 59
Spooner 16
Spradling 6, 24
Spralling 32
Spurrur 73
Stallcup 10, 31
Stallions 19
Standley 46
Stanfield 22, 60,
  69
Starck 73
Stephens 64
Stark 18, 21, 45,
  49
Starks 38
Steele 53
Stenson 51
Stephenson 17, 24
Stevenson 13
Stewart 1, 9, 11,
  22, 35, 41, 52,
  55
Stone 39, 44, 61,
  70, ... 73
Stovall 37, 45,
  50
Stowens 25, 26
Stratton 41, 49,
  59
Street 9
Strode 51

Strother 3, 7, 13,
  17, 52
Stroud 19, 49
Stubblefield 39, 46

Suit 60, 61
Sullivan 16, 46, 51
Summers 19, 38
Sute 74
Sutton 5, 72
Swaney (Swanyney)
  35, 41, 43, 44,
  67
Swann 19
Sweat 40

Talley 55
Tannon 2
Tarbury 5

Tarron 49
Tathum 1
Tatum 41
Taylor 8, 13, 19,
  25, 26, 29, 51,
  54, 65, 68, 69,
  71, 74
Teasdel 71
Teely 40
Telsinger 38
Tendall 37
Tennie 72
Tenney 15
Tennon 3
Tensus 58
Terril 3
Tesdale 72
Therborn 22
Thomas 22, 51, 66
Thompson 2, 3, 9,
  13, 17, 59, 68
Thrower 73
Thurmond 47
Tilly 32
Tinn 10
Tinnin 9
Tinnon 3, 11, 14
Tison 56
Todd 10
Tomblin 32
Tompkins 15, 22
Tossly 29
Townsend 33, 39
Tracy 75
Traber 38

Trail 17
Tribble 49
Trice 13
Trigg 13, 19, 25,
   26, 44, 45, 47
Trousdale 8, 28
Trulock 7
Trumbo 16
Truble 24
Tucker 75
Tullock 8
Turentine 64
Turnbul 20
Turner 19, 30, 38,
   56, 57, 58, 60,
   63, 69, 71, 72
Tyler 50, 51
Tyree 40, 49

Uzzell 24

Vance 52, 63
Vardiman (Vardimin) 28
Vaughn 69
Vinson 33, 56,
   16, 22, 29, 61

Vormington 18
Wagoner 29, 50
Waldrum 48
Walker 49, 50, 54
Wall 3, 6
Wallace 3, 20, 31,
   27, 63, 68, 74
Walldrip 6
Wallis 63
Walton 6, 11, 13,
   31, 38, 39, 46,
   57, 58, 53, 60,
   63, 68,   72
   71
Ward 44
Warrington 13
Washington 18, 23
Waters 19
Watkins 28, 56,
   72
Watson 18, 19,
   63
Watwood 65, 74,
      75
Weakley 11
Weathered 50
Weatherford 71
Weaver 18
Webb 22, 32, 62,
   63, 73

Weems 9
West 51, 69
Wherry 44
White   13,
   15, 25, 26, 27,
   30, 32, 33, 38,
   49, 59, 69, 70,
   75
Whitsett 2, 3, 9,
   13
Whitworth 8, 25, 26,
   49, 72
Wilkerson 43
Wilkins 59
Wilks 33, 39
Williams 2, 3, 4,
   10, 16, 17, 28,
   32, 35, 39, 45,
   47, 52, 54, 56,
   65, 67, 68, 70,
   74, 75
Williamson 37
Willis 6, 7,
   22, 42, 43, 46,
   67, 60
Wilson 2, 3, 4, 5,
   9, 11, 13,
   17, 18, 20, 29,
   30, 31, 44, 51,
   54, 55, 62, 63,
   66, 67
Winbourn 59
Winchester 3, 4, 5,
   6, 20, 23, 41,
   50
Winhaw 65
Winstead 67
Winston 64
Wisdom 9
Withers 6, 8, 50
Wood 6, 13, 45,
   47, 62
Woodall 59, 68
Woodruff 54
Woods 75
Woodson 33, 56
Wootton 18
Worthington 43
Wright 13, 25, 28,
   46
Wyllie 61
Wynn 25, 26, 33
Wynne 33, 52

Yandall (Yandall) 7,
   9, 10, 15, 18

Youree (Yourie) 16,
   24, 25,   , 73
Young 5, 15, 35,
   47, 73